Let's Talk Polo

LET'S TALK POLO

For the polo player...things you need to know

SUNNY HALE

A personal note from the author…

Let's talk Polo…for the polo player, is the first book released in a series, for people who want to become a better polo player at any level of the game. It covers the essential things you will need to know about how to actually get it done. Including all the details that nobody explains, the stuff that takes years to understand and usually takes 100's of chukkers to discover. It is straight forward, to the point and easy to follow. The techniques and strategies are proven and are what gave me the chance to play as a professional for and among some of the all-time greatest polo players in the world.

I hope you enjoy the book and this first conversation about Polo. We may have a few more, but the intention of this first book is to help those of you who have a passion for playing polo with some insider details to improve yourself as a polo player that you won't find anywhere else.

Here is what I learned along the way in pursuit of my dreams in the sport of Polo.

Good luck,

Sunny

CONTENTS

CHAPTER ONE

Let's do this...

So what's the secret to becoming a better polo player?

Welcome to your first step in becoming a better polo player by buying this book. Now step # 2 will be to read it. Whether you just started or have been playing for years, what I am going to share with you in this book will give you a roadmap to follow in achieving your goals to improve as a player at any level of the sport. The techniques and strategies are proven and are what gave me the chance to play in 22 and 26 goal polo as a professional for some of the greatest players of all time with the longest winning records such as the legendary Carlos Gracida, Memo Gracida and the world's #1 polo player Adolfo Cambiaso among others. To be a great polo player you must truly be a student of the game and especially be open to having your ego run over a few times so you can learn new things.

The most important thing to determine in becoming a better polo player is, what are your goals in the sport? It's important to first determine what you want to do, because it's a huge menu to look at and take in when you first start. Once you have the answer you can get to work on the next steps to doing just that. It's important to define your goals as a player, because to be the best you can be you will need to know what you see for yourself. Once you know what your destination is, you can start attacking the details, but if you don't see your destination you will struggle with realizing improvement and will plateau on a regular basis, because you're on a path with no defined destination. You know, kind of like being lost in the woods… the trees are beautiful, but where's the path to the cabin?

The importance of a polo player's mind: Sorting it all out as you go is the key to making progress and becoming all you see for yourself in the sport. Therefore, be ready to keep an open mind because your strategies and approach to things will change as you progress. It's important to recognize that the knowledge and strategies that worked when you started will evolve into a well-oiled machine of dominance, as you understand different concepts to the same tasks. It often takes years to understand that each level of polo has a different concept in the strategies for getting the same tasks done depending on your knowledge and skill level as a player. For example in low goal polo when you start, you might be told to "go ride off your man and make sure to always ride him off on his or her right side". As you progress to higher goal polo you will be told to take a man, same task, but be expected to know how to take him or her so you own the inside of the field in the process and that may not always be the right side of your opponent. Each time you jump up to the next level, you will not only be opening up a whole new thought process, you will be challenging yourself to a new set of expectations and adrenaline level full of new interests. So be open to this thought and remember I said that, as it is one of the most important aspects to recognize if you want to improve and keep the confusion to a minimum. If you always keep an open mind for what you yet don't know, you have the best chance to becoming as good as your potential. All of the skills and elements that make up the sport of polo and a great player must work in unity to become the best, so pay attention to this fact. One skill won't make you great, but a well-rounded approach to understanding and being able to execute them all as you progress, will. Finding success mentally with each small step you make in progress will open the doors to new to opportunities and new thought patterns about your strategies.

It is also very important to learn the art of "not biting" to the pressure of the game and losing your focus to fouls, opponent banter, bad plays and personal mistakes for this reason. With each one of those topics that you decide to "bite on" and get frustrated, lose your sanity, scream out some new obscenities is one less percentage of energy you have to having your best performance. Think of your energy and mindset for the day like a wallet of potential. You have 100% to spend loaded in the wallet. If you spend 40% of your wallet on frustration, now you only have 60% left to spend on having a good game, real simple. Act like a complete whining idiot for a few chukkers over a certain play gone wrong or persons actions means you just gave away a few chukkers towards having your best performance. Always remember this fact: a polo player's mind is the key to his or her goals in the sport. Often times a player who has a solid and calm mind at any speed can overcome another player who has superior skills, but a weak mind and here is why. All you have to do is turn the heat up and watch the player meltdown....yeah...it's the key to finishing games when you sense the crack in the opponent's mind. Then you just fill the crack with more frustration until the game is yours because of their errors committed out of frustration and a drop in concentration. The trick is to keep pushing the buttons until the crack you've created by frustrating one opponent, by getting them to "bite", becomes a disease to the entire team. Once the crack is too wide to fix...game over. Did I tell you yet that I love strategy? Strategy of the mind during a game is one of my favorite topics in polo at any level. One of the most important things to recognize is that you will need to train your mind as you go, to handle the pressure until nothing can make you bite. Keep conditioning your mind until all of your energy stays focused on these replacement thoughts: the next play, what can I do to get to my man quicker, what can I do to not commit that foul again, what can I do to help my team better on the next play...keep at it until these become your new natural default reactions to pressure. Being able to have this kind of a mind that doesn't bite under pressure drives opponents off the deep end...fact.

Always be open to creating an environment to continue growth. Think of it as a garden...if you do not plant the seed, nothing can grow. You must challenge yourself continuously along the way, whether it is a jump in goal level of a tournament you usually play or choosing a harder opponent to mark or trying to play a new position...find what challenges you and give it a try. Making this a habit to live by, no matter how small each challenge you choose may feel or seem in the overall picture, will take you step by step to becoming a better polo player. Whatever you have found that gives you confidence, you should continue to use and if you aren't improving at the pace you would like, then start looking for the reasons why not or look ahead to new challenges that will pull you forward. There are so many elements that are tied together in becoming the best polo player you can be. Therefore it is extremely important to give time and efforts to absorb as much as you can and to understand how they all work together to make the complete package of a good polo player. This book will cover some of the key elements to incorporate in a well-rounded approach to improving on a consistent basis, such as improving your Stick n ball habits, practice game logic, preparation for tournament games, horse management and the basic ingredients that make up the Language of Polo to name just a few.

Now for the hard to hear news. Always examine your game losses and try to get to the right answer about why it happened. Yeah, it's not always pretty to look at, but it is the answer to improving so do it! This is the greatest gift you can have, to find the gold nuggets in the rubble and be willing to do the work it takes to solve the issues that caused the loss is what all great sports and competition is about. So be open to figuring out what are your mistakes and what you can do about always trying to correct them before the next big game so you can have the best personal performance possible. Yes, looking at your mistakes is hard, but I guarantee you this...once you figure them out, you will stop repeating them and your game will start to elevate for sure. This is probably the most important personalized aspect of improving your skill as a player. It is what makes the great players great...they work at it. It just so happens that this line of work is extremely fun, but don't tell anyone!

Now let's get to it. There are several topics in this first book like polo ponies and strategy that truly need a book of their own to cover properly, so stay tuned as the book series is released. But for now, each chapter I've included in this first book about how to become a better polo player is a summary of the foundational stuff you will absolutely need to give time and energy to if your goal is to be the best polo player you can be. Each chapter can also go extremely deeper in depth in thousands of advanced details from the text that is there, so if you are left wondering at any point...is there more...good news...there's lots more to know ☺. What this first book released in the Let's Talk Polo book series contains, are the absolute foundational tools, concepts and thoughts you'll want to know that usually take hundreds of chukkers, fouls blown on you or lessons before someone finally explains it all. So always keep that thought in mind as we go. Now let's get started!

And p.s. ...if no one has ever told you this before, polo is addicting and there is no cure ☺...you were warned!

CHAPTER TWO

Stick n Ball...

The importance of creating good Stick n Ball habits

Stick n ball is about preparation, learning to be prepared for all of the shots that may be needed on the field. One of the hardest things to do when you go stick n ball is to actually leave the stick n ball field with something more than just exercise and here's why. When you stick n ball most people go out with the idea that more time in the saddle with mallet in hand hitting balls, will produce a better player in the next game. That is not actually always true. Yes more time in the saddle with a mallet will help familiarize you with it all, but have you ever had an amazing day on the stick n ball field only to hit your next game and can't seem to repeat any of what happened on the stick n ball field? Don't worry you are not alone. This happens to most people. What will produce a better player in the next game is to figure out what you are missing or is difficult in your ball striking capabilities and then each time you go to the stick n ball field attempt to work on one or more of them until you have achieved the understanding and skill it takes to repeat that shot from anywhere. This takes time and practice so don't think it's all going to happen in one day.

It is the use of this thought pattern that will start to build your confidence. Use your stick n ball time to try new and difficult things that inspire you or are difficult until you master them one small step at a time, shot by shot. This is how you create your pathway to the top of your handicap in terms of your ball striking capabilities. My point, don't leave it to chance if your hitting will all of a sudden get better in the next game. Go work at it and determine what you want to master and then get to it. By preparing yourself on the stick n ball field to be able to perform all of the shots, you are giving yourself a greater chance of pulling them off in a game and building confidence in the amount of tools you will now have in your toolbox when you go to the field. The idea when you go to the stick n ball field is to find something that you are going to work on and spend a portion of your time that trip to the stick n ball field on that one topic. Once you feel you have hit a few shots well and can repeat the shot you are working on then move to something else. Adding this habit to your stick n ball routine even if its only 5 minutes of your overall time spent that day, will open a whole new level of confidence as you master each little success. This is the best way to prepare yourself into having your next best game in your hitting abilities. Having a purpose when you hit the stick n ball field will help lead you to being a better ball striker for sure.

Get to the stick n ball field as often as possible. It is important to think about the frequency you actually do get to go stick n ball. Is it every day? Is it once a week when you go to the club on the weekends? Do you stick n ball only right before big games? These might sound like funny questions, but there is a real reason behind them. The frequency of your stick n ball and what you practice when you are there will determine the rate of your improvement as a ball striker. Maybe you are like many who get to play in the summer months only and then have no access for the winter months due to 10 feet of snow! So you have to wait all winter thinking about your polo and what you will do next season to improve. Answering this question will determine a lot about how often you will have the opportunity to improve on your ball striking abilities and just how important it is to effectively use your time when you do go. My point, take a look at how often you have a chance to improve and then get to using your time wisely if you are serious about being a better polo player.

A couple of simple questions to ask yourself that will change everything about your stick n ball results. There is no exact science that works the same for every player on how to improve, but one fact that will always help you when you go to the stick n ball field is to pay attention to the small details, including the hidden ones.

❖ **Who is the stick n ball session for?** Yep, you read that right. One thing that is always helpful in producing better results when you stick n ball, is to determine before you go out the answer to this question: Is this session for the horse or for myself? By that I mean, is it to improve some of your hitting skills or is it to exercise the horse or give it singles time? Or is time for you to get to know the horse or gain confidence in it? This is really important to decide as most days that are spent in useless frustration and that don't lead to much in improvement are the days you are trying to improve your hitting while riding your most difficult horse, with no idea why you aren't improving. It is always a good idea to spend more time in the saddle with mallet in hand building confidence in your horses, but if you truly want to improve your ball striking ability which is what stick n ball is really for, then you will do yourself a favor by knowing which horses you have in your string or access to that will provide the best platform to work on your hitting. I mean specifically the ones that give you confidence. These are the horses to make it all about you and really leave the stick n ball field with a sense of getting something accomplished and building your confidence in the process. This will help put a stop to those days you leave the field completely frustrated on how your hitting was that day. Remember this statement. Each horse you get on has something different to offer. The point is to

26

recognize which horses you have, or have access to, that will give you the best chance to work on "you" and "your hitting skills" and then recognize when you are on those horses it is for you ...all about you. When you are on the difficult one, or one that does not like to stick n ball, or is green, be aware that this horse is not the best environment for improving your hitting skills and therefore this is not the horse to worry about reaching your hitting perfection on. When you are on that type of horse, be a bit more forgiving of your hitting mistakes in place of attempting to work the horse as he or she needs to be worked to improve its performance for you in the next game and your ability to get the most out of it. Challenge yourself to find confidence in some part of it, but keep in mind that trying to co-mingle the two ideas may result in frustration and a possible drop in your confidence, which is completely counter-productive. When you actually think through this question before you go out, you will get a much more productive and enjoyable experience leaving the stick n ball field and this is what improving is all about. The best afternoon or morning is the one spent galloping in the sun on a beautiful day and fun horse enjoying the time practicing, but it is the attention to the fine details and correcting what holds you back that will make you a better ball striker. Being a better ball striker is a key element in improving your overall ability as a polo player.

❖ **What is your construction zone?** Ok, it's just me and you here…let's have it. What is your biggest glitch? Everyone has one. That shot or maybe there are a few of them that you rarely try because of how difficult they seem to pull off. Here is where we can start to cure that glitch or issue. Stick n ball is about time spent learning what you need to do to improve on the things that are the hardest for you to do or can never pull off consistently. Building confidence that you can execute your shots when called on or at your discretion randomly is the key to becoming a good ball striker and here's why. In a game you don't get the freedom of an empty stick n ball field with no one screaming at you and no one demanding the need for you to "HIT IT", "TAIL IT"…"WAIT, HOLD IT"…and then a loud whistle when you hit a ball that was "apparently" not yours. In a game, there is no peaceful afternoon gallop by yourself chasing the ball wherever it lands. Each shot you get the chance to hit must be delivered somewhere defined immediately and usually in a very small window of time. That is why it is important to make a mental list of your most difficult shots and start to think of them as a "new construction zone". It will take time to complete the project, but by asking yourself which ones stick out as the biggest issues, you will now have your own personal list of what needs to be worked on. Spend some time each stick n ball session on improving one or part of one until you master it. If you need help with specifics ask a pro or take a lesson or go watch a lot of games and pay particular close attention to the player you most like the hitting style of. Then see how that player makes the shot you are having difficulty with. You don't need to spend the whole session frustrating yourself and it is not recommended, but you should give a portion of time each time you go the stick n ball field to improving one particular shot or attempting to start trying it. This is what will pull your game forward and help you improve. Once you hit a few good ones on the topic move on to something else or back to a bit of what you are good at. This will give you a well-rounded approach to adding new tools to your toolbox of shots and start to build confidence in new areas.

Create targets and challenges for yourself. It is important to recognize that for each shot you think you have mastered there is always a way to challenge yourself to increase the amount of options you have with the same shot. For example, if you think you're good at neck shots try hitting them at more severe angles until you can hit a target that is actually behind you on the left side...see what I mean? It is also important to always create targets for yourself that you are actually shooting at as you move around the field. Actual targets or a destination you are carrying the ball to, will produce some pressure as you hit the ball and that's exactly what you need to do to simulate game pressure. The only way to train your mind and reflexes to act together rapidly with accuracy is to practice that exact skill until it becomes second nature to be able to execute a shot exactly where you had in mind in a split second decision and it actually goes there! Stick n ball can also be done and is the most fun when paired up with a friend and attempting to pass the ball between the two of you as you round the field, calling for shots as you go just like you would in a game with your team mates. This drill can be super beneficial especially when you guys have a destination you are carrying the ball to and actually finishing with a shot on goal or to the intended target.

No matter what you choose to work on, it is important to try to get the most out of your stick n ball time as possible. If you want to improve your ball striking capabilities in a game, give these drills and challenges a try next time you hit the stick n ball field. Good luck and I warn you now…some of them will leave you completely disturbed at first so keep at them until you can do it ☺!

* **Improve shots on goal and concentration: the slam-dunk drill.** Set 3 balls up as if you had to hit penalties at a goalmouth. One on the 60 yard line (centered just like a penalty shot), one on the 40 yard line (centered just like a penalty shot) and one on the 30 yard line (centered just like a penalty). Now, make sure the balls are set up in a

straight line centered in a line directly to the center of the goalmouth and then here is your challenge. Make one large approach headed to the right on the right lead as if you are going to take the 60 yard penalty shot, only this time you will hit all three balls with one single approach ...yes, canter down the line of balls and see how many you can get in with one easy swing at each ball. The 60, the 40 and the 20...all at a steady slow canter and NO turning back and NO second loop. If you miss one...too bad, keep going to the next one. Repeat the drill until you can make all 3 balls in the goal without missing and without speeding up or swerving all over the place. **Benefits:** This is one of the BEST drills to use to help you improve several issues such as 1) your accuracy shooting at goal under pressure 2) being able to hit that second or third ball while running and 3) determining your hitting technique issue based on the spray pattern of your balls where they end up. This is the drill to cure those issues. Once you are able to do the drill where you can actually make all three balls in with an easy swing at each one, step it up a notch and really try and kill the last one or try moving the balls closer together for even more pressure.

❖ **Build mental confidence in carrying the ball consistently: Circle drill.** See if you can carry a ball, using tap shots or short cut shots, in the shape of a circle to the right. Yes a nice big circle and not just any size your horse chooses, but actually map out in your mind how big it will be and then try to carry the ball all the way around the circle without missing. When you can do it once successfully, now try to go 2-3 times in a row. Yes, without missing and without a huge change in the size of your original circle. **Benefits:** helps hand eye coordination, helps build wrist strength, helps simulate game pressure in executing a task in a defined space, helps build mental confidence in your ability to turn the ball successfully.

❖ **Build confidence hitting under pressure: Two tap shots then hit away.** Put your horse in a nice easy canter and attempt to take two small tap shots (a tap shot meaning your hand starts below your horse's back, this is a placement shot and not meant for distance) in a row and then attempt to hit the third shot at the ball with a full swing. Your third (away) shot needs to happen at exactly on 3 not four, not five and not on the next loop...that is the whole point. Creating pressure to hit away in a defined number of shots. **Benefits:** Be prepared, because at first you may be completely flustered...LOL...and that is exactly the point. To recreate what happens in a game. You know, that moment when you all of a sudden hear "HIT IT!!!!" and you immediately shank a ball or completely miss it... yeah that one. This drill is for that issue, being able to pull off an accurate shot under pressure. Use the tap shots for ball placement. Repeat it until it feels smooth and there is no stress…well, major stress that is. If you master this one really quick then add a target that you are hitting the third shot to.

❖ **Improve confidence carrying the ball at speed: Destination at speed drill.** Start at one end of the stick n ball field by teeing up a ball and then pick a destination at the other end of the field, an actual point of reference (it could be a tree, or a goal, or a fence post, anything that you can gallop to) that you will be galloping to with the ball. Once you are teed up and ready, put your horse in a steady gallop on the right lead and head off in a large circle at a controlled canter headed to the right. Using a full swing hit the first ball away then attempt to maintain a ¾ speed gallop and carry the ball to the left side edge of the stick n ball field and then to the end of the field ending up at your destination point. Attempt to drop the last ball exactly where your spot is. If you should miss a ball on the trip, do not stop, just slow your horse down circle to the right back to the ball and then move back up to your ¾ speed and keep going. Very important is to learn to maintain a consistent speed, don't let the horse dictate the speed. **Benefits:** helps get you comfortable to execute finishing a destination you have in mind, helps get you comfortable when running and hitting under the pressure of a defined goal with all of your shots. PS…get ready to miss a whole lot of balls the first few attempts due to the added pressure put on your mind to arrive in an actual destination with the ball. This is the whole point, so stick to it until you can do it no matter how slow the bits of progress seem in the overall picture. Even if it's only one successful run the first time you try it out. Next time it will be 2 successful runs and then you're on your way to running with the ball successfully in a game. It is this intense pressure in the game that destroys your ability to concentrate on the task of running successfully with the ball. Practicing this drill will help you to overcome that pressure you feel in a game.

Ok, now for some good news!

The importance of recognizing your strengths on the stick n ball field: It is important to recognize what you are good at and there is a very important reason why. What you are good at provides the basis for the go to weapons when you are playing in a game. When you have confidence, you have the ability to challenge yourself in spaces others will not go and take chances others will not take. This ability is what makes a great player great; they can go places other players don't dare. To catalog what you are good at will help you define where your confidence is and where it is lacking. When you need a day of stick n ball to build confidence go out and practice really hitting your mark in the things you are good at, but be warned, the things you are good at will also deter you from improving if you choose to only repeat them when you stick n ball.

When you ask most people what they are good at they will hesitate for a moment and then after a moment or two of reflection will come up with a couple of shots they feel ok with. It is rare that someone has perfected all of them, so your job is to discover what you are good at and then make a list of what else is left. That is how you will get better, to go after time in the saddle on the stick n ball field practicing the things on "the rest of the list". Let's call "the rest of the list" part of your construction zone. When you throw in a few rounds of what you are good at between sessions of confusion and struggle to reaffirm your confidence, you will start to see an improvement in your overall skill and confidence. This is stick n ball time well spent.

How do you improve on the things you are already good at? Start to challenge yourself in a new way with the same shot. For example, if you are really good at distance hitting with the offside forehand...try shooting at targets and a specific distance to increase accuracy. Here's another one, for back shots try increasing the angle of your back shots and actually attempt to shoot them at a target behind or to the side of you. This will build a wider range of areas that you are capable of delivering a pass to. With each shot you are good at there is always another level of skill you can achieve with it. So once you think you have one mastered find a way to challenge yourself further with it. Always have a destination in mind with each shot you are attempting to improve on.

How to get the most out of your stick n ball when it is, "all about you." Line up the horses and figure out what you are working on. Really pay attention to your technique and executing shots for accuracy before distance. Really challenge yourself to push your boundaries of comfort zone to start working on shots that are difficult. Use the steady horse to work on that nearside that is driving you nuts. Use this time to work on your full swings and distance. Use this time to work on running with the ball, knowing you are confident on the horse and can shut it down anywhere if things get a little wild. No matter what you choose to work on, make sure that when stick n ball is all about you and the horse is all confidence, know that this is the time to really pay attention to improving your techniques, your style, your abilities...it's all about you, pick some topics and go for it...this is your time.

The importance of productive stick n ball time to a polo player: Each level of confidence in ball striking gives you a new outlook to what you might want to try on the field in a game situation. That's why it is so important to find what is working in your stick n ball routine and keep at it. Over time these small improvements will add up. If you never challenge the stuff that is difficult or off limits you will never know the power of confidence. Without the power of confidence, you will always have doubt going to the field, which leads to limitations that you are painfully aware of when you play. The way to remove doubt in the shots you are having difficulty with, is to practice them in a controlled environment on the stick n ball field until you feel you have mastered them. Even if you have to break them down into single elements of the shot as a whole until you get it put together, this is how you improve.   Attack each new challenge, as you are inspired to feel brave enough to try it. Practice games and the tournament is where you find out if you have mastered them yet...or they are still under construction.

The best players in the world did not get there because they stopped at what they were good at. They had to spend hours on the stick n ball field finding that edge that gave them superiority and the discovery of new skills along the way. They never settled to only look at themselves, they always are searching through watching and playing for the skill that outdid them in the last game. This is where the real work is done.

The discovery of what you are missing and the pursuit of building confidence in those areas, through constructive stick n ball time, is how you build quality stick n ball habits and improve your overall skill level. A player with excellent ball striking capabilities can do things the average player can't, because they understand how to overcome pressure, execute delivering passes in small spaces and can finish goals. This is why it is important to become a good ball striker and it is done on the stick n ball field. So make a mental note what you are good at, be proud of it…then reach around and pat yourself on the back and get over it. Get back to working on the things that are not on that list. That's how you will become a better ball striker.

The key to great stick n ball is finding the balance between what you are good at and what needs work "the construction zone". So start putting some of these ideas and concepts in motion in your next stick n ball session even if it's one particular thing that sticks out to you that you read and see where it leads you. Once you start to see a way to actually predict improvement by the steps you are taking yourself, you will now be on the road to knowing how to become a better ball striker on a consistent basis. This ability will bring a new level of confidence that will open new opportunities in your game choices and new things you will be willing try because of your new level of confidence. This is the key to progress at any level of the sport. So now that you know how to do it, get to the barn and pick out a horse and get started!

CHAPTER THREE

Practice Games...

Quality practice takes organization

Practice games are about finding things you need to work on as an individual player and using the time to really find your confidence in executing them. What it should not be is a place to just log hours repeating the same ole routine that leaves you asking...where's the beef? Here are a couple of questions and thoughts to always keep in mind to get the most out of your next set of practice games. With the right preparation you will have the best chance to really get some work towards becoming a better polo player done in each practice. Here are a few new thoughts to add to your arsenal of improvement tools that will put you on the path towards more productive practice games.

❖ **How often do you get to practice with a team?** This is a huge and important question to answer. Practicing with a team is a huge benefit, but not everyone gets this opportunity. Practicing with a team usually is done before or during a tournament with an organized plan of attack. The reason it is a great benefit is because you get to start with a defined position and therefore know what the basic idea is of your positioning on the field for the day. This gives you some parameters to work with as a start point. Your job then becomes to play the best position you can. This is the organized approach to practice and the most beneficial. Without this basic default place to start yourself in, a lot of practices become a random selection of positioning and most times with little or no communication as there is no defined plan you are following and no defined wrong place to be. When practicing in club practices that happen usually bi-weekly around the world the routine is the same. You sign up, you have no idea who will be your teammates and you show up and do your thing. You may not even decide really who is playing what position and you may never ask who you should mark...do not worry this is the norm! Unfortunately many good chances at really improving are lost in the shuffle of practices that just roll out without a plan and before you know it the game is over and you left the field without feeling satisfied. The way to get more out of practice, is to start asking your random team mates that are better than you, questions such as "which man do you want me to mark", or "what position do you want me to play?" These basic questions will now give you some tasks to go to work on. You will now have a clear and defined job for the day and can get to work on doing the best job in that position or in marking that particular player. To create some kind of destiny or plan in your practice game is to give yourself the best chance of getting the most out of practice and improving your game. To understand the difference of practicing with a team or a plan versus random mix up practice and running the wheels off your horse with no improvement is to recognize how much opportunity to improve exists in each practice. How much you get out of it depends on how much of a plan you had going in.

❖ **Each practice needs a title. Are you practicing for yourself or your horses?** This is a huge question to ask yourself and should be asked with each practice and here is why. When you go to practice, the most common mistakes that lead to horse injuries or ruining good young horses is mixing the point of the practice up between who it is truly for...you or the horse? This is also a large factor in players lowering their handicap unconsciously without even knowing it for this reason. Playing green horses is all about what that horse needs at that particular stage of the training process and how well it is accepting the input of info. The player then has to ride defensively, which means the seat changes from hanging all over the place in the ready to hit the big ball on any side at a split second's notice, to a deep rooted deep seat with feet forward to prevent getting dumped or that random side-hop that's always fun. What happens over time is the player begins to have hitting issues because they are no longer in a ready for anything over the middle of the horse position. Instead, they are in the defensive driving position of the back seat hoping to be able to sort through random surprises, as all green horses produce especially in practice. Over time this affects the player's confidence and they may not realize where the issue is coming from. A player should not bank on being a superstar in the chukker he or she is training a green horse...just focus on the horse's needs and always remember to readjust your riding position back to game mode when you go to your made horse. Here is another common example of why this question is important to answer...horse injuries. It's early in the season and you go too hard on a horse who hasn't been in work too long because you just had to keep up with the speed of the practice and who was out there that day. The horse is now injured and maybe out for a good portion of the season all because you forgot or never asked yourself the question...is today's practice for me or the horses? The other common issue in injuring horses is bringing a good one back that had an injury and now you are out there on the practice field and the game lights up and you know you can make some superstar moves on this horse because this one gives it all and can kick butt around the other horses out there. So you go ahead and make the moves and haul ass before the horse was truly ready...re-injured. When the practice "is" about both of you together, is when your horses are fit for the season after being properly legged up and it is time to put the two together and see what you got. Until that time, the practices are about moving the horses and you getting back in form as well, but in gradual increments as you both are ready. Knowing who the practice is for and at what stage of fitness your horses are at will help keep your string healthier and your game performance in peak of confidence condition, because you will know the difference of when you are taking it easy and when you are pulling the trigger on the full package of you and your horse. Getting horses ready for the season does not mean that in all practices you can't hit a ball or have some fun, it just means you need to be conscious of what the purpose is that day and know your limits with the horses as they need them to be set. This will ensure the best longevity in their career and give you the best chance to play your best polo, because you know when you can push them all the way. This over time builds confidence in the player as well because while you are practicing you know you have a few more gears. The question is, can you be patient to use them?

❖ **To be a great player, you must conquer at least one position.** Over time as players become seasoned they will all find a certain position on the field that they truly enjoy and feel comfortable at depending on their abilities and thought patterns. You will do yourself a big favor to try and figure out what is your best position for your playing style and abilities. It may change as you progress, but it is a good idea to start figuring it out so you can be the best at at least one of them. A really top player can play several positions well, but it is a rare commodity for sure.

❖ **How often do you get to practice in the same team position?** This is an important question to think about, because each time you practice you have the chance to improve your ability to play a certain position or work at improving a certain skill of a certain position. Most people don't break it down or think of it in this kind of detail, but your use of a practice game even if it's a throw together mix of players is key to improving your handicap. If you can completely understand each position or have the best knowledge of the one you most like to play, you will then have the best chance of getting the most done in a tournament situation and enjoying a game. To know exactly what you are supposed to do, when to do it and where to line up to get the most out of the attack is the aim of learning your position. If you practice and repeat the same behavior each time and do not look for something to work on, such as a certain position and trying to really cover all the needs in that spot...you are shorting yourself the true value of "practice" and need to ask yourself this question...what am I actually doing out there besides just reacting? Don't worry, it's just us here and I won't tell what your answer was. Being a better polo player is about learning how to become the move maker, the deal breaker, the play buster and the one that the other team is complaining about. If there are better players on the field, ask their advice how you can be more effective in that position. You may be surprised to know most good players are very receptive to help with the answers. Also, always remember, each player has their own opinion of what's best, so choose a player you actually respect the moves of…just saying. Also, try this…if you sign up for club practice often and as in most clubs it is a random mix of who gets paired with who and therefore no way to plan ahead, try to round the bases on positions if you feel you have hit a plateau in improvement. Ask your team mates for the day, "hey, do you mind if I play # Four today or this chukker?"…if you usually play #One. The reason is this. As you try other positions you will immediately begin to understand the mistakes you have been making as you watch the player at the other end of the team commit them, only this time you see the mistake because you needed them to make a certain play so you could have a play on the ball. The other way to practice is to play one certain position each time and really do your best to master it. Ask for help from better players on the field if you think you are missing something or get confused. This is how you learn to become a better teammate and improve your ability to play a certain position very well.

How to get the most out of practice games when you are on your own, with no "organized team practice". Here are a few thoughts to start adding to your practice routine that will help open up more room for improvement.

❖ **Challenge yourself against better players.** How often do you get to practice with better players? This is a huge question to answer, as practicing with better players although frustrating at times is the only way you can truly improve. They will challenge your skills, your ego, your true talent and your ability to improve. Without the challenge of better players you will become the largest fish in your pond. Strive to find the better players on the field and challenge yourself against them and match yourself up against them even if it's only in club practice when you get the courage to use them as the person you will attempt to mark. Only seek one out when you feel confidence to give it a try and for sure don't go grab the highest rated one first time out of the box and ask for your butt to be handed to you in a to-go bag. Be nice to yourself and start with someone who is just a touch better and attempt to mark that player. When you feel some confidence you can do it fairly confidently, then move up a notch and pick a tougher one in the next practice. Improvement comes by being challenged. This is the way you move yourself up the ladder in game skills and the way you grow the tolerance of your ego, which will always determine your ability to improve or become stagnant.

❖ **Determine a goal for the day.** What is your purpose? This may sound like a funny question and an even more obvious answer, but there is real value in determining exactly what this practice game is for. Of course it's to practice, but the question is practice what? Are you there to practice the horses just to move them? Are you there for a team practice to get to practice team plays and positioning? Are you there because it's Thursday and you signed up for practice and that's the normal routine? Are you there to try horses? Are you there to get more time in the saddle and on the field? All of these answers are valid, but your knowledge of the answer to yourself before you get there will determine the amount of benefits you actually leave the practice field with. To define each time you go the field what exactly is your purpose or goal to work on that day is to give yourself the best chance of a speedy improvement in your game. If you give yourself a purpose for the day or a goal to try and reach in the practice, whether it be marking a certain man, owning the center of the field in your ride offs, backing the ball to a team mate instead of turning it...whatever you feel you want to work on and maybe there are multiple small things...if you get them in your mind before you start, you will have an excellent chance to make some serious improvement. When you give it a shot to try and execute one or more challenges you have set for yourself, you will find true enjoyment in the time spent and walk away feeling a bit accomplished in adding some new confidence on the field.

Here are few options to try in your next practice game to challenge yourself:

- ❖ Work on playing a certain position that you want to master, than focus on it.

- ❖ Choose one person you will mark for the game, make it someone above your handicap.

- ❖ Work on shooting for goal when you get within 60 yards, from all angles instead of tapping.

- ❖ Try playing in a new position.

- ❖ Attempt to own the center of the field each time you mark an opponent during a knock in.

- ❖ Try to win all of your ride offs by getting your knee in front of your opponent's knee "before" you make contact with them.

Take some time when you're headed to your next practice to map out trying one or more of these concepts or details I have shared with you and watch your game take a whole new turn. Good luck!

CHAPTER FOUR

The Language of Polo...

The unspoken structure to all great polo games

Polo is played all over the world and I can attest to this fact, that in my travels to play in 11 countries so far and at all levels of the sport, no matter where you have learned to play, no matter what country you play in, you are going to eventually run across the 5 most traditional strategies and concepts that make up the universal Language of Polo. These 5 basic elements are the key ingredients to how a polo game will most likely flow around the field. It's like being in a canoe and floating on a river, if you know which way the river flows and don't get in its way by paddling in the wrong direction. The higher up the handicap of the polo, the more simplified the polo looks at speed, because of this language that everyone seems to speak fluently and the riding skills of the players. The lower the level of polo the more confusing the game looks from the side, because not all of the players have had enough education or game experience yet to truly understand the basic elements that will make your game flow at its most fluid capacity. Knowing and executing the Language of Polo, to those who know what they are looking at, shows each player's respect for the unspoken language executed among real teammates who are willing to work for each other on the field. This is what bonds the members together as the basis to grow everything else from that they might come up with in strategy options. Below are some of the absolute "must knows" of polo that are usually only discovered in small tidbits after years of polo and years of making mistakes with someone breathing down your neck yelling out these terms that just don't make sense, or an umpires whistle over and over…well here's what they are trying to tell you.

The five basic elements that make up the Language of Polo: These words, phrases and basic concepts are what structure the order of all great games and are what make up the Language of Polo, so pay close attention. These are the most important things to know when trying to understand the order and flow of a game and are universal throughout the world no matter what country you are playing in or language you speak. These are the oldest traditions in the way polo is played and has been played for generations.

<u>ONE:</u> **The phrase Man-Line-Ball.** If you take your **MAN** first…then the **LINE** should be yours…the line leads to the **BALL**. This has to be **the most important concept in polo**…most important…so pay attention to this part, it is everything to becoming a good polo player. This is your get out of jail free card for all tricky situations. This is the flour in your pancakes. This

concept means that when you have a choice to make on the field, you should always make the choice in that order: Man-first, Line-second, Ball-third. And especially when you are not sure or totally under pressure and don't want to commit a foul. Always keep this concept in mind as your "default" answer and counselor for all questionable situations. Especially the ones where a better player is tempting you to foul by launching a ball out in front of you and you're trying to decide if it's yours or not. Tattooing this sentence on your forehead is a good idea until you get it ingrained in your mind and it starts to occur as a natural reaction. Man-line-ball is the safe default answer to any and all questionable situations. To break it down even further for a really clear understanding you have to think of it in this order for these reasons.

More insider details and the reasons why... Man-Line-Ball in that order:

❖ **Why Man first?** Always go to your man first and establish contact with them to win a better position to be on the Line. Winning the position on your man will give you possession of the line in almost all scenarios. Once you have taken a man successfully, 9 times out of 10, you will have the right to the line and to take possession of the ball. Without winning the position on your man and completely taking their play on the ball away from them first, you are playing with fire if you go to the ball they were hitting and most likely will be committing some type of foul. This is the play that never makes sense. You know, the one where a player behind you hits the ball right passed your stirrup a few yards and then you take the bait and SHAZAAM the whistle blows...crap, I thought I had enough room...yeah that one. Always choosing to wait and go take the man first, will start to help you win that play you used to lose or foul in. So start thinking Man-first in all plays where there is a ball that is lurking out there all alone and you are wondering if it could be yours. Look for the man on the line, or the one who hit it last and go establish yourself in his or her face and take them out..."man first"...then the line should be yours...the line leads to the ball.

❖ **Why Line second?** Learning to go the man first is always a better choice, because going to a line means nothing if there is already someone established on it that owns the right of way. As you become an experienced player you will be able to read who owns the line much better and things will become really clear as to when it's ok and safe to take a line from someone and when you are committing a foul for sure. But this takes years to learn how to read properly and when it is ok to pull this off. And remember this fact, the fouls in a game are called at the umpire's discretion and each umpire may have a different opinion of the event, as each one is a unique human being with their own experiences and interpretations. Crossing the line in front of someone who appeared to be completely behind you or out of the way will be like a recurring bad dream until you get the concept of man-line-ball. Here is how it works: someone was bringing the ball down the field and is established on the line and therefore has the right of way. In order for you to successfully (meaning you do it without fouling) take the ball from them, you must own their line and the only way to make sure you own their line is to completely take them out in a ride off first...thus, MAN first. You can go to as many lines as you want, and absolutely think you got their first...but if there is a more seasoned player at the end of that line well established on it (who therefore owns the right of way), they may have just set you up for the most fun sucker play! Which will result in a penalty shot and some extra yards for free when the whistle blows on you for fouling. Don't fall victim to this manufactured foul anymore. Oh yes, every good pro knows this little trick to pull on unsuspecting new or inexperienced players. Help yourself by changing your thinking and your default answer when you are not sure what the right move is to make. Going to the line first and thinking the ball is yours, because you got their first or because your horse was faster or the ball went over your head passed you is setting you up for a potential foul being blown on you. This is why going to the man as your first option and then the line properly as your second option in the list of choices is absolutely important, especially if you want to start opening up plays you never knew existed. It is the formula that will serve up the most improvement in your ability to really get things done on a polo field as opposed to just being out there and wondering why you aren't ever the playmaker…you are always the one just reacting to people. This is why. Learn to execute this concept and it will change your game forever.

❖ **Why Ball third?** This is the simplest of concepts yet the hardest to incorporate for most people, because everyone's natural instinct is to go after the ball first. In fact, most people's biggest flaw to solve in becoming a better polo player is to stop watching the ball. When you are focused on a ball, you are not focused on your surroundings and the storm of offense or defense that is brewing around you. Going to the ball first is a sure fire way to get the umpire to start using that new whistle. Going to the ball first means you are running the risk…HIGH RISK…that there is someone else that has just hit the ball last, that actually still owns the line and you are asking for a foul by not taking them out first. Going to the ball first also means you are leaving a man free on the other team. If you miss the ball, that man can become your worst nightmare as they are free with no one on them and you will now have a huge amount of yards to cover in trying to catch them before they do real damage. When you go to the ball first in a play you are unsure of, you are setting yourself up for the lowest percentage odds of pulling off a great play for the team. You may get away with it a few times, but that will only breed confidence in a weak play that will eventually cost you dearly if you keep repeating it against better players. In fact, as a professional player this is one of the most fun plays to pull on unsuspecting new players in a tournament situation. Yes, you read that right…the secret's out…totally entertaining maneuver! To just lob a nice ball out a short way in front of an unsuspecting player and then sit back and watch them take the bait. Foul, free yards for me ☺! This is really fun, especially if someone thinks they are just going to do it quicker the next time…bring it on. The idea is to keep forcing the error in this flawed strategy of thinking until you completely frustrate the player and they stay away from you all together or you win yourself some free yardage in the form of several nice short penalty shots. So please, if you learn one thing from this book, learn the mistake you are making in going to the ball first, it can be a costly one.

TWO: The words… "BACK IT!" Learning the importance of backing the ball instead of turning it is a huge part of becoming a good polo player and a good team player. Why you ask, is this a better play

61

than keeping it yourself and turning it? Backing a ball will keep the flow of the team's offense going and lessen your team's chances of losing possession through a failed attempt at turning. Every time a player chooses to back a ball they are setting up a much more fluid defense, the strongest chance at an effective offense and building confidence in operating as a team instead of a pack of individuals. Each time a player attempts to turn a ball, they are giving the opposing team an opportunity and maybe many (depending on how many taps it takes them to successfully change directions) the chance to steal it, the chance to be hooked, the chance to foul if done improperly and the worst case scenario...the idea that a team is one person. The best polo in the world is almost seamless to watch because every player out there understands the concept of backing the ball as the key element to trusting and working together as one cohesive unit. When executed correctly, a back shot will give you the best chance of covering the most yards in the least amount of time. This is why the best games look so smooth. Backing the ball sets up the best offense, because of the amount of yards that can be covered in a well-directed back shot to a team mate who is already turned in the other direction to receive it. The second and extremely important reason it sets up the best offense is the amount of defensive players that can be left inside the pass with no play on the ball, if the shot is well executed. This strategy can have a huge effect on reducing the opposing team's opportunities to gain possession.

Winning a polo game is about maintaining possession of the ball so you can have more opportunities to shoot on goal. This is why you want to skip weak plays that cause a team to lose possession and opt for the play that has the highest percentage odds of producing a good result for the "team".

Now for the good news, if you are completely addicted to turning the ball. This does not mean that you should never turn a ball, ever again. My point is to teach you that the rule of thumb in the language of good polo is that backing it should always be option #one for the reasons stated above. When is the right time to turn a ball you ask? When all of your teammates are covered up with a man and can't get free, then you may want to turn it to maintain possession until someone is free to receive the pass or maybe you have to bring it yourself. That is the exception to the rule and should be considered as option #two in your line of thinking. In that scenario it is better to maintain possession than to back it to no one or worse, to the other team.

THREE: The words…"TAIL IT!" Tail shots are the most important back shot to learn to execute well and there is a huge reason why. Hitting a well-executed tail shot sets up your teammate to gain possession of the ball and have his or her hitting side completely protected. When you back a ball straight back, you give the next person in line that was behind you a chance at possession and that person may be your opponent...yeah, rutro. When you back a ball "open" or "away" you have sent a pass to your teammate that may meet with head on opposition from someone who was following behind you...once again your opponent. The tail shot sets up a play for your team that can stay in fluid motion once the pass is received. The other two options are high-risk moves that can create a traffic jam of people who now may potentially have a shot at owning the line. Using a tail shot will open up your game by knowing how to set up a successful offensive attack, especially when you are experienced enough to execute it with a man on your hip...double play!

All over the world, using a tail shot shows your experience and your skill level no matter what language you speak. This is one of the key elements to the language of good polo. It does not mean that you should never use all of the other back shots, but what I am saying is that it is of utmost importance to understand why the use of a tail shot is so important over the other options. The tail shot will almost always provide you with a good chance at a new offensive attack for your team and is key to understanding how polo flows naturally when done right. A tail shot is a key element in the Language of Polo, because it sets up the protected pass. The protected pass is your catalyst for a solid start to an offensive run.

FOUR: **The concept behind hitting a Knock-in to the right.** Here is a huge clue to how most set plays will start...huge insider secret known by the top players all over the world. About 75% of all knock-ins and penalty #5's from the center of the field will start to the hitter's right and here is the reason why. Knock-ins can be sent in any direction that the hitter feels is best to reach the intended receiver. But the reason knock-ins and penalty hits from center will almost always be hit to the right of the hitter is for this one simple fact...to protect the hitters or receiver's right side (hitting side) when they receive the pass.

When a knock-in is hit to the left side of the hitter, the hitter (if they bring it themselves) or the intended receiver will be carrying a ball to the left side of the field with their hitting side (right side) open to be hooked by an opponent. When a knock-in is executed to the center of the field or the left side of the field it is a much riskier plan, because you have now given the other team a good chance to come in and steal the ball or stop the receiver with a simple hook, which means possession over. This is why 75% of the time when watching games you will see the play go to the right when it comes to knock-ins and penalty hits from the center of the field. When you understand this basic concept in polo you will now have the ability to read most situations no matter where you are playing, as with most experienced players you can count on this play to unfold even if you can't communicate with them through speech.

An additional benefit of this knowledge is this. As a member of an offensive team who is bringing the ball in play, you will know what they know and they will expect that you will be heading in the most sensible destination to receive a protected pass...to the right. As a defender, you will now know that there is a 75% chance the hitter is looking to hit to the open receiver that is headed "to the right". This knowledge sets you up for some pre-meditated moves and success in shutting down weak plays. See what I mean, there really is a Language of Polo.

Having this knowledge sets you up for success in planning an early attack because you already know the odds of what will most likely happen. A good premeditated strategy is the key to all great victories.

FIVE: The concept behind the word **"TEAM MATE"**. Teammate is the one word that can spell complete ignorance in your performance and ability to speak the Language of Polo. Now we're getting into some top-secret info!! This is one of the simplest secrets to know in polo that is unspoken, but absolutely part of the language spoken among all top professionals who are scouting potential young talent. Does the player know the value of playing as a "team mate" and executing the role of the position or number he or she is playing, or do they run around showboating their ball skills and cool moves stick n balling all by themselves warming up? All flash, no cash situation = no job for you young professional. A real polo player (even a ball hog) does know the value and importance of functioning in a designated role and how much each player depends on you to cover your position, even if it's not the most glamorous task for the day.

I can attest to the fact that some of my most fun and challenging jobs playing high goal polo had to do with trying to "execute exactly" what I was asked to do as a teammate. Many times I was asked to just keep a ten goaler from seeing a ball that day, or please keep the ten goaler away from our ten goaler…"k…I'll get right on that". You know, the kind of job that doesn't have a defined place to be, but should end up with you taking your mark to the hot dog stand on the boards for lunch, because that's what your team mate asked of you and they were counting on you to do your part so they could do theirs properly and free of attack. Sometimes in high goal polo I was given a certain jersey number, but it had no meaning as far as what role or position I actually played.

The role was determined by the needs of the team captain and often times it meant just filling the gaps of defensive dirty work to create open spaces for the ten goal player to do their magic.

So don't fall victim to thinking you are all alone on a polo field. No matter what the handicap level of the tournament and the skill level of your team mates in battle, you will always play better when you are willing to make plays for and with each other as a team. If you think about it, these are the games you come out of feeling the best about regardless of your win or loss result and here is why. Whether you won or lost, being a real teammate is the idea that you were all in the same battle and your backs were aligned in the same direction as one. This is a huge component to being able to speak and execute the Language of Polo. To learn the value of being a teammate and making plays for the good of the team and the play you are trying to win as a group. Even the best players in the world need a supporting cast to win.

The benefits of being able to perform the Language of Polo in your actions when you play: When you are able to understand the language it doesn't matter how fast the game becomes, you already know what the basic layout will look like and what to expect. Then the fun becomes throwing in a few strategies to mix up the norm and what is expected to catch opponents off guard.

It's when you do not understand or have never been taught these oldest traditions in polo that the games will all seem random and really hard to predict what is coming. Take the time to think about this the next time you play and watch for the patterns I am talking about in this chapter and you will start to notice some real coincidences in all the great players. This is no coincidence. It is the Language of Polo in motion. All great players know how to speak it, even if they can't communicate verbally because of an actual language barrier.

The Language of Polo is spoken all over the world through generations of polo players and exists in all good polo games you will watch. The fun in traveling and playing polo is meeting new friends who share the same passion and speak the same language on the field. That is when playing polo truly becomes another level of fun and competition. So make it a habit to start incorporating these basic concepts to your game and watch your world on the field start to take a huge change in perception and what to expect. Knowing how to execute these concepts when you play, also demonstrates your knowledge of classic traditional polo...or lack of.

CHAPTER FIVE

Tournament Games…

The importance of tournament games to becoming a better polo player

Tournament games are the place where you find out if all of the work and fun you've been having at the polo club is paying off or needs some adjustment. You can play all the practice games you want and think you are really good, but until you put yourself up against other players in a tournament formula you have no idea what you are missing. Tournament polo is where the heat gets turned up a notch and your skills will be put to the test along with the skills of your string. What I have lined out for you in this chapter will give you an overview of the most important things to always consider in tournament preparation, including how to do your personal best and the importance of finding your mistakes.

As you progress as a polo player, always keep this thought in mind regarding what level of tournament polo you are playing and how often you play tournaments at a different handicap level. You will find that with each additional step up in handicap level of tournament you are willing to enter, you will be climbing the ladder of knowledge and skill level in polo. Each rung on the ladder that you go up, will produce a whole new level of adrenaline, challenges and pressure to perform. This is also the reason why when you drop back down a handicap level or two in tournament handicap level, the games don't produce as much pressure or stress on you as they used to. You feel like you have much more time to make plays. This is your mind in the process of learning to expand your game skills. This is how you become a skilled polo player over time.

Preparing for Tournament games. Success in winning and having your best personal game performance starts with the basics of good planning and organization. It is extremely important to realize that for each task you have to give attention to on game day and especially right before or during a game, is one less space you have to focusing on your personal performance in the game. To be organized when you go to polo is not only necessary for an enjoyable day, it is absolutely essential to becoming the best polo player you can be. Being organized means being organized at the trailer, being organized in your game help for the day, being organized with your horses for the day, being organized with your tack, being organized with your team, being organized when you actually lay out your personal game gear for the match. It means being organized across the board in all areas and ready to go.

When you organize yourself appropriately before each tournament game you will have much more room to concentrate on the game at hand and that is what it takes to truly get all of your personal abilities to top form. The more space you have in your mind to concentrate on playing your best game, the better off you will be in your end results as a player. Each level of disorganization is one more distraction that causes a delay in your ability to improve.

How to do your personal best

Here are some things to always keep in mind when preparing for tournament games. These thoughts and actions will help you get your focus where it needs to be, so that you can have your best personal game performance.

The importance of organizing your horses before you get to the field: Making sure your horses are well organized before you get to the field will ensure your greatest chance at having your best game for this reason. Each segment of concentration it takes to solve a horse issue that pops up on game day is one less place in your mind you will have to concentrate on your actual game performance. This is when poor choices will happen, due to the limited space of time and energy to solve the task at hand with a well thought out plan. Having the right line up and having the horses arrive at the field comfortable and quiet, can mean the win or loss of a game. Any distraction on game day is a distraction from your ability to give 100% of your energy towards your personal game performance. If you are tacking for yourself, it's even more important to get things organized before the game as you have a way limited amount of time and energy since you are the groom and the player.

The importance of making the best horse line up for yourself. You may want to start assessing how you line up your horses. There is a real advantage to being conscious of where you place a horse in the lineup and here's why. Each horse brings a certain amount of confidence to your game or a certain amount of doubt. Where you place the horse and the point of entry that they come in can sometimes determine the win or loss of a game. Have you ever watched a game and could completely see the difference in horsepower of a certain player whose horse really cost them or won them the chukker? This is the reason I am pointing this out and why it's so important to attempt to make the best horse line up possible with a well thought out plan.

A horse line up can also be made for the fitness of your string and managing horses to survive a long season. What is most important is to determine what is best for you and the type of string you have currently. There is no wrong answer, so just give attention to what gives you the most confidence in each horse and how you will line up your bullets so to speak, so you can hit the target of a personal best each time you go out. When you give some serious thought to how you will line up your horses in advance of getting to the field, then all you have to do is to get on a well thought out plan for each chukker.

What you can get done on a horse can sometimes mean sealing a victory or one more long thoughtful drive home because one chukker of poor planning. Give this some thought and see how you can start to line your horses up so they give you the best chance at having a great game.

The importance of warming yourself up before the game: Do you have a strategy or thought pattern about warming up before the game? One of the most important things you can do for yourself is to get your mind ready and open for just polo. By taking a few moments before the game to go out and hit a few balls, you will give yourself an outstanding chance to have a good game performance. The reason for this is that you will have a chance to get your riding and hitting rhythm going and get into your confidence zone before the first ball is thrown in. This will also give you a chance to get the jitters and kinks out. You will in essence have a head start.

For those of you who get extremely nervous, this is a great way to calm your nerves and get some breathing going. Entering your first chukker calm and ready to speed it up is what you are aiming for in your warm up strategy. If you have a warm up strategy that gets you in game mode, keep it up. If you have never really had one, start looking for one that gets your mind ready to concentrate on the game at hand. For some it is horseback and for others it is with some physical activity, stretching or that drive to the field with your favorite music playing. Either way, you will do yourself a big favor if you give some thought to a good strategy for warming up before you play. The last thirty minutes before you enter a polo field can often determine your mindset for the game. Make it a valuable last thirty minutes through warming up or getting in a place mentally that you can focus on your game ahead. This is always a good strategy to improving your game performance. Getting your mind focused is the key to getting everything you can in physical talent to perform at its best, so start paying attention to this small, but huge detail and see where it takes you.

Some valuable horseback warm up routines:

❖ **To get you started in the right mindset of scoring goals and loosening up.** Take a ball from one end of the field to the other making a point to actually go through the goalmouth at each end at least once. This will get you thinking about finishing goals and using the whole field. Don't worry so much about your technique (that was what stick n ball time was for), just worry about your "destination" through the goal with the ball and enjoy the time getting in your groove. This should be done at the pace of a nice easy canter.

❖ **To get you started in the right mindset of scoring goals.** Set up a few penalty #2's. Hit two or three shots from the 30-yard line just to get your ability to focus and pay attention going. This will also put a little pressure on you to pay attention to finishing your goal shots and where you are actually hitting the ball, instead of just long distance random shots that feel pretty. Make sure to aim your horse through the middle of the goal and follow through with your swing to a spot you have chosen behind the goalmouth as your target you are shooting to, such as the scoreboard or a tree or the flagger's bucket of balls ☺.

❖ **To get you relaxed and to start having direction with your shots.** On one of your routes down the field, make yourself carry the ball to each sideline with long easy shots. This will help you open up your field vision and calm any last minute nerves. Focus on your destination with the ball, instead of your technique and how it feels. This should be done at the pace of a nice easy canter. You may also want to throw in a few angled back shots with a target in mind to get the edge off so your first game shots can be good ones.

❖ **For the advanced player: To give you some pre game pressure and get your focus going.** Make one to two of your routes down the field at half speed and finish with a shot through the goal. The idea is not distance, the idea it is consistency and rhythm in your riding and hitting.

What to do if you get nervous before games: Give yourself a focal point to really put all your attention into, such as your task for the day in who you are marking or the position you will be playing. It is extremely important to get your mind right before you enter the field to make room for a great performance. Also, make sure to go out for a few minutes of stick n ball or riding time on the field before you start to get your breathing going and loosen up. Most players who get really nervous also spend the first chukker so tight that they hardly take any deep breaths and therefore get extremely exhausted very quickly.

The point in what I am explaining about warming up is that when you go ahead and do something to get yourself warmed up and the pregame jitters gone, you will now have a shot at actually fully participating in all of the chukkers right from the first throw in. Instead of spending the first one to two chukkers calming down and starting to breath...leaving you only a few chukkers left to actually give it your all mentally and physically. So find what works for you in a warm up plan and then start applying it so you can be best prepared for your potential best game yet.

Turning losses into victories: the importance of finding your mistakes. Always examine your game losses and try to get to the right answer about why it happened. This is a direct roadmap to what needs to be fixed to do better in your next performance as an individual, as a team and as a horse owner wondering about your string performance. This is the greatest gift you can give to yourself. To find the gold nuggets in the rubble and be willing to do the work it takes to solve the issues that caused the loss is what all great sports and competition is about. So be open to figuring out what are your mistakes and what you can do about always trying to correct them before the next big game so you can have the best personal performance possible. Yes, looking at your mistakes is hard, but I guarantee you this...once you figure them out, you will stop repeating them and your game will start to elevate for sure. This is probably the most important personalized aspect of improving your skill as a player, it is what makes the great players great…they work at it.

Start implementing the parts of this advice that apply to your current interests and you will be amazed how much more you will get out of yourself. Good luck!

CHAPTER SIX

Polo Ponies...

The key to being a good polo player

Polo Ponies are a tremendous source of pride in any polo player and a topic I am absolutely passionate about. In fact, it is the reason I created the American Polo Horse Association to recognize and document the great athletes of our sport. It is also a huge topic to cover properly and for that reason it will get its own entire book as the Let's Talk Polo book series is released. What I chose to cover in this chapter on polo ponies is information I know to be vital for every polo player to know or learn at some point in their career about polo ponies.

It takes years to perfect a successful routine in any venture you will take on in life and having great polo ponies is no different. One of the greatest passions to share in, as a polo player, is the connection between you and the horses you will have in your string. Confidence is the key to pushing your limits as a polo player at any level of the game and good horses are what will give you that confidence. So if you take only one thing from this book, take this fact. Good horses and knowing how to ride and care for them are everything to being a great polo player. So take the time necessary to become a good rider, a good horseman and learn all you can about how to care for these amazing athletes who are the heart of the game.

Buying Polo Ponies

How much should I pay for a polo horse? This is one of the biggest mysteries in polo. All over the world polo players and sellers have the same issue at times in trying to figure out what a polo pony is worth and why. Some of the most common guidelines people like to use in determining a dollar figure for the horse are the level of polo it is capable of playing, its soundness, its age, its glitches on the field, its experience, who owns it, who has played it, its breed, and its pedigree if known. Polo horses also sell for all different prices depending on if you are in or out of season in your area, who the seller is, what club the horse is being shown at, how easy the horse is to play and what the economy is doing as that will also affect buyers spending limits. Yes those are all good guidelines and helpful tips in price negotiations, but the real answer is this…true fact. A polo horse is worth as much as the buyer is willing to pay and how much the seller knows in marketing their horse. That is the real answer. That is why you hear of a horse that was bought by a friend for $3,000 and it is amazing and a horse that sells for $200,000 and it is amazing. To each owner they have what they were looking for and are happy with the price they paid.

The horses that sell consistently and are worth the most money at any level, are those that are safe, consistent, sound and easy to play by anyone with lots of options, so don't be fooled.

What differentiates a good low goal horse from a good high goal horse and the price accordingly, is how many options to perform it has to offer the player, just like buying a solid car. Each car you buy will most likely get you down the road, but you will pay more for the car that has more options like speed and handling capabilities. It's that simple, so don't let the smoke screen of the unknown and fancy chatter deter you from using your common sense in determining the right price for you to pay for a horse. Buying a polo horse and the price you decide to pay is up to your budget for a horse and how much value that horse brings to your overall enjoyment and experience as a polo player. There are general guidelines and acceptable going rates for horse sales within each club you will spend a season at, so pay attention to what the market seems to be determining in horse sales and then make your best efforts to use your common sense and not be misled so that you can come out with the best purchase possible.

Important terms to consider when purchasing a polo horse: When you are considering a horse for purchase, here are some terms to know to sum up a polo pony's experience and potential value and a few things you may want to ask the seller to better determine what type of horse this is. It's always a good idea to ask a lot of questions, because horse-trading is one of the oldest industries and you will do yourself a favor to listen closely to the answers. One of my favorite horse tradin' stories is about the guy who goes to buy a horse from an old horse trader and the old horse trader says "the only thing is, he don't look too good" and the buyer goes "I think he's beautiful, I'll take him." Turns out the horse was completely blind and didn't…"look" too good! Honest horse trader.

I have done myself in many times with some fantastic mistakes, so here are a few details to pay attention to when you need to understand better what you are looking at in price considerations for a polo horse purchase and experience of the horse you are considering. Buying polo prospects is a whole book of its own as there are many factors to determine in purchasing the right prospect and how to go about it, but this brief overview should help you improve your buying habits when it comes to polo horses that are already playing. All of these details can be factors in what you will actually receive in the horse you purchase and in the potential price negotiations to a positive or negative effect. It's always a good idea to pay attention to the small details to ensure a good purchase. Making good purchases will help you increase your enjoyment when you play. It will also help you to become a better polo player over time with a better quality string that suits your personal needs.

- ❖ **Green horse:** term used to describe a polo pony prospect that is not fully trained for polo. Green can refer to many stages of the training process, but usually means is not ready for tournament polo. Keep in mind green horses need time to become finished "made" horses and rushing the process by adding tournament polo too soon in their career can ruin their ability to be a really solid steady chukker.
- ❖ **¾ Made:** refers to a polo pony that has had many practice games and maybe a few tournament chukkers. Generally speaking a ¾ made horse is ready for a professional to start introducing to tournament polo on a regular basis to complete its training. It is important not to assume a ¾ made horse is the same as a "seasoned made horse".
- ❖ **Made horse:** term used to describe a horse that is fully trained and ready for tournament polo.
- ❖ **Seasoned horse:** term used to describe a "made horse" that has several polo seasons of tournament polo under its belt in experience.
- ❖ **For safety reasons: Cinchy, girthy or cold backed:** These are the terms used to describe a horse who has an issue when it is saddled and may include bucking, flipping over or laying down if not managed properly when being tacked up or mounted. Always ask the seller if this horse has

91

any of these issues described above and here is the reason why. Those issues can be extremely dangerous to a rider and take a trained professional to manage properly. Therefore, you may be best not to take the personal risk in owning a horse with these type vices...so always ask.

Buyer's Guide

What to buy: for the new player or potential horse owner. What type of horse are you looking for? Becoming a better polo player is all about the courage to try new things that might at first scare the living daylights out of you, but leave the after burn of the rush of a lifetime in your bloodstream. Therefore, the most important thing to keep in mind when buying your first and second horse are these two words…safety and confidence. The most important thing you can gift yourself when you start the sport of polo is to get the right horses under you and here is why.

Safety is issue number one for this reason. If you put yourself in an unsafe situation with a horse you have just purchased, because of pressure to pull the trigger, you have potentially shortened your life span and have secured many insecure chukkers to come. Do not purchase a horse until you feel completely confident it feels safe and has no vices that will put you or your family in jeopardy. To worry each time you go to tack it up or enter the field that something wild is coming or you don't have the ability to shut it down anywhere on the field, is to delay your ability to become a better polo player in exchange for becoming a defensive driver of a 1,000lb animal through the traffic of 7 other people running around you. Now, what is the quickest way to skip that mistake? Pass on any horse that does not feel safe to you...yes you. No matter what the seller says, it is you who will be riding and playing it and you who will ultimately pay dearly if it is the wrong horse. The mistakes made when first entering polo can be expensive if you do not follow your gut instincts and common sense when it comes to purchasing polo ponies, especially when you are a new rider as well.

The second most important word to consider is confidence. What kind of confidence am I talking about and why does it matter? The confidence you are looking for is the difference you will feel immediately. Yes, I said immediately "when you first throw your leg over a horse". The horse and you will either hit it off and you will feel like you could go anywhere on this horse or, you will immediately feel questions...lots of questions...and each time you get on it you will feel more questions. Pass on the horse that gives you too many questions, at least for now until you get more experience to be able to assess it fully. Questions don't always mean it's a bad horse, it just means it may not be the right horse for you right now and you will do yourself a large favor to pass for now until you know more and can make a confident solid move in the area of purchasing.

If you take the time to make the right purchase on your first horse and it is safe and provides confidence, there is always a market for this type of horse when you outgrow it. This will also give you some return on your investment should you decide to sell the horse at a later date. Always consider older horses with a lot of game experience as a high priority in the line-up of suspects and potential options for your first purchase or two. This type of horse can be the fastest way to truly get started in the sport, because their experience will help you get to plays in complete confidence that you may never have considered with a young spirited steed that you were just trying to stay on top of.

Always remember, it takes years of experience for a polo horse to become a truly "made" and "seasoned pony" with tournament experience. There are always exceptions to the rule, but in general you are always safer to go with a horse that has years of tournament experience as a starter horse. If you are looking for a horse to help teach you the game, make sure it has had a lot of polo and it is one you feel complete confidence in, nothing less.

What type of horse to buy: for the seasoned polo player and string owner. The best way to assess, which is the right horse for you to purchase, is to first determine a "benchmark group at the top" from your current string that you would love to have more of. What I mean by "benchmark group at the top" is the single horse or horses that you absolutely play great on and wish you had more of. Answer this question to yourself. Which horses in your string fill this thought? "When I leave the field all I am thinking about is my game and everywhere I went". Immediately when you read that last statement, you probably had one or two horses pop into your mind. Those are your best horses, because they allow your focus to be on improving your game. It is that horse or those horses that we are targeting for the sake of this exercise. They are your benchmark group at the top of the string. Those are the kind of horses you want to have more of in your string and here is the reason why. When you play those horses it's all about you and improving your ability to play good polo and that is the mind frame you need to be in to improve your polo. Any chukker you play that the focus is not on that, is slowing your personal progress as a player. Making the concept of "buying a horse that is comparable to the benchmark group" as a default counselor in your buying practices, will help you to stay on the path to an overall better string. Now get to work on building your string to include more of those kind of chukkers.

When you have great horses you will feel invincible on the polo field. Feeling invincible means you will be willing to try new things you never had the confidence to try before, because of horse limitations or insecurities in the horse you were playing. If you really want to speed up your improvement in the game, then you should pay particularly close attention to this advice on improving your string.

One of the biggest downsides to not using this concept I just explained above when buying horses, is also the largest factor that leads to creating a string full of so-so horses by accident. Let me explain why. The way a lot of horses are bought usually goes like this. We all get caught up in a season and all of a sudden you have one or more horses out for an injury or stupid setback and you are a bit short at the moment and here comes an opportunity out of the blue to grab up a "useful" horse that will get you by for the season while the others come back. Before you know it you have bought 3 or 4 of those type horses, over a couple seasons and are topped out on the number of horses you want to own. This will stunt your growth as a polo player for sure. And don't worry you are not alone. This happens all over the world to players at all levels of the sport. In fact, ask yourself or any polo player you know this question: how many of your horses do you ABSOLUTELY LOVE to play? Then ask them how many horses they own in total. What you will find is most people own a bunch of horses, but only a couple they ABSOLUTELY LOVE to play. Dare ya…ask a few people and see what you find out. It is a common issue in holding players back and for this reason. Most people buy horses at random times within a season and usually to fill a gap or an immediate need instead of an organized approach to improving the string as a group over time.

Once you have determined your "benchmark group at the top", you will now have an idea what kind of horse you play your best on, what kind of horse you are looking for and who he or she needs to be able to measure up to. When you are looking to buy horses, you are looking to expand your ability to have great chukkers more often with more of those horses. When you take the time to implement this purchasing strategy in first identifying the benchmark group who are doing that in your string currently, you will have an excellent indicator of what you are shooting for in your next horse purchase. Then the next biggest step is to be able to have the patience to wait until you locate exactly what you are looking for...this is the trick. This thought pattern and habit will help improve your ability to play your best more often, which leads to solid improvement at all levels of the sport as a player.

And always remember this...it costs just as much to feed an enjoyable horse as it does an imposter who drives you nuts. If you are a new aspiring polo player, so not to be fooled, a mediocre horse will give you mediocre ability to get around the field.

In your new purchases, you are looking for a horse that compares to the benchmark group of your top three horses, or if you want to really get serious, it must compare to your best horse. That is how to choose the horse that is right for your next purchase and over time using that as your strategic buying guide will produce a better overall string. A better overall string will lead you on the quickest path of opportunities to becoming the best polo player you can be, because of the amount of places you can go on the field when you have confidence in your horses.

Making your own polo ponies vs purchasing made: some tips for the "do it yourselfers". Good news, I've been there done that many times so here is the low down on buying a prospect and training it yourself when you are trying to be a polo player. I have enjoyed the absolute pleasure and passion in the journey to the next great prospect and literally spent years in the process of hunting the countryside looking for prospects to add to my string in every imaginable scenario from beautiful farms, to last chance opportunities like the weigh pens at local auctions, to people's backyards, out of the newspaper classifieds, fresh off the racetrack to the unique opportunity of training a race horse that had won a million dollar race to play polo successfully. So when it comes to horse stories and do it yourself knowledge of purchasing, training, selling expertise, huge mistakes to avoid…watch out I got a whole bookcase full of fun stories. Here's the low down. Anyone can dress up a horse in polo pony clothes and get them to gallop around the field and act like they play polo, but the trick is can you actually produce a horse that is suitable for you and that truly becomes a value to your string? This is what professionals spend years perfecting their talents at, so be prepared to make a few mistakes and give yourself enough time to do a good job with your prospect.

Keep in mind that the most common mistake in trying to do this yourself if you are not a professional horse trainer, is to make the assumption that you will produce a finished playing horse exactly when you need it. Green horses need time to complete the entire training process and the necessary time to become a seasoned pony through practice and tournament games. The cost of that horse by the end of the process which can take from a few months to a couple years, depending on the individual and your ability to read the needs of the horse, is the cost you just paid for that horse...add it up.

There are ways to get a horse to play polo really quickly and that is by knowing what to buy and where to go to locate that kind of talent, but that is a whole book in itself. The idea is to always keep in mind that if you want to take on a green horse to make yourself, don't assume this horse will be a starter right away. Make a point to enjoy the journey as this horse will bring you a lot of satisfaction if you get it made, but you have to remember each time you play it and until it is completely made this one thought that all true professional horse trainers know… EVERY SINGLE chukker you play it is for the horse, and not the player. Whatever the horse needs at the stage he or she is at and NOT for you. When you try to mix the two ideas is how you ruin a good prospect and how to bring your handicap down in a hurry. I am not saying to avoid the fun of making horses, as there is so much satisfaction in the process and the journey, but what I am saying is to be realistic about the costs and about the needs this horse will have that need to be attended to on a daily basis to bring out the best in the horse. That is if you want to produce a really good one. This single point I am making, about giving a green horse the proper amount of time and attention, is the single largest factor why there are a limited number of truly top horses to be bought due to the fact that people get in a hurry due to finances or inexperience and try to rush the process. My point is this. If you do decide to do it yourself, make sure to factor in the proper amount of time it will take. This way you can give enough personal attention to teaching your prospect all of the details that build the necessary confidence in a young horse. This approach will give you the best chance at a truly great polo horse.

This can be one of the most fun and enjoyable experiences when done right and one of the absolute greatest sources of pride when you play a top horse that you made yourself. So if this is your passion, make sure you pick a horse that you are capable of working with depending on your skill level.

For some additional brief advice to the aspiring polo pony trainer, here is a thought process to live by when purchasing prospects to train and sell as made polo ponies. Always buy a prospect with an end result of the guesstimated potential sale price you think that horse could bring when finished out and ready to sell, as well as what level of polo you are aiming for in mind, before you pull the trigger on the purchase. This will ensure the greatest chance at a serious profit and make your time and effort worth a financial return, which will keep your business around for a long time. Make no mistake, top seasoned made polo ponies are hard to find and needed at every level of the sport, so do your best and you will be on your way to becoming a seriously popular person in the world of polo.

Riding the Polo Pony

Polo Ponies are the heart of the sport and will carry you to your greatest victories and hardest defeats. They will be with you in the battle every step of the way and if they trust you they will give you their heart and soul to help you be your best. No matter how good you are as a player, you can never outdo the value the horse will bring to your game in a positive or negative way. For this reason you will do yourself a favor to try and be the best horseman and rider you can be, in your search to be a better polo player.

Why is it so important to know how to ride for polo? Learning to ride properly for polo is what will give you your best shot at being safe in the sport of polo. Learning to ride well for polo is also what will give you your best chance of getting the most out of a horse that it has to offer. Consider this fact. How well could you do if you were placed in the driver's seat of a massive submarine with little sea or boating experience? How much do you think you could know about its capabilities in just seven minutes and would you be able to max out its capabilities submerging, floating and ascending? Or try this example. What would happen if you were thrown in a high level race car and had just seven minutes to figure out all of its gears, special features, speed capacity, safety options etc.

before your race started? How much of the racecar's full potential do you think you could get out of that car when the race started? Well, this is why it is so important to spend time off of the field to learn all you can about riding your horse properly. Not only is a horse complex, it has a brain, emotions and a heart that can all translate into a bonus jackpot of help or a complete ass and saddle fight if provoked in the wrong direction. So do your homework and start spending some time on the track practicing or taking a few extra lessons if there is a polo or riding coach close by who inspires you.

For those of you new players wanting some help in the riding for polo department, here are a few riding drills to try away from the game to help you log some hours towards having stronger riding capabilities when you play. Remember this, the more time you spend riding the more confidence you will be able to attain.

❖ **Strengthen sport specific riding muscles by taking a set:** A helpful pre-season riding drill can be to go take a set with your groom or a friend who has polo ponies. This exercise will help you start building your riding muscles and help you learn to pay attention to your surroundings and more than just you. This will broaden your ability to be confident in company as well. Early preseason trot sets are also great for building and strengthening lower back and sport specific riding muscles, which work as a very defined group when playing polo.

❖ **Practice riding with a partner and being able to stay together as you change speeds:** Just like when you mark a player in the game, practice keeping your horses shoulder to shoulder as you ride along and attempt to change speeds and even practice coming to a full stop or changing directions as a pair that stays in sync. The idea is to be able to keep your horses proceeding at the same pace in sync as you maneuver around the track or practice field. You might even try some circles for some added pressure to keep up and pay attention. For this exercise it is not necessary to actually crash into your riding buddy for a full ride off. The goal of the drill is to be able to stay even in accelerating and slowing down until you are able to make the transitions smoothly and without losing your buddy in the dust as you ride along.

❖ **Practice changing speeds on the track or practice field.** Take a pony out and give some time practicing the moves and riding skills you will need on the polo field. Practice starting from a walk and accelerating to a gallop and then coming to a complete stop after a few strides. Then try changing gears from a slow canter to a gallop and then reducing back to a slow canter. The goal of the drill is to be able to change speeds smoothly and without losing your balance. These can be drills you try out on the track or stick n ball field where you can truly concentrate on just the riding portion and getting things to where they feel really comfortable and can be executed with confidence. A helpful tip to add pressure and an added degree of difficulty to the drill, is to pick a spot that you are riding to and then attempt to change gears (speed) at exactly that spot.

Riding habits to correct that could be affecting your swing and skills on the field. One thing to always be paying attention to when you practice riding for polo, is where your riding hand is placed as far as height. Here is why. When you have your rein hand too high it throws off your entire hitting platform and leaves you off balance when you go to swing. The proper placement for your rein hand is to bend your arm in front of you at a 90 degree angle at about belly button height and then attempt to keep it at that general height when you ride and stick n ball. It can go forward sideways, up when the head goes up to go with the horse, but it should never be kept at or higher than your chest as a lot of people will do to balance themselves. This may sound funny to some of you who are experienced riders, but the truth is, hand height effects many seasoned players natural ability to swing a mallet correctly. So take a minute to evaluate where your riding hand placement is the next time you ride ☺, you might be surprised to see what you discover.

Another detail to pay attention to is how long you hold your reins. Holding your reins too long slows down your reaction time regarding the horse's movements and can make you late or leave you off balance when you attempt to hit the ball.

Also pay attention to this riding question: are your reins a third stirrup that you use for balance or a tool to help you guide your horse? If you answered yes, they help me to balance myself on the horse, then you will need to practice weaning yourself off of this habit ASAP and here is why. This habit may also be affecting your ability to get around the field efficiently and your ability to really hit a great ball. Yep, hitting the ball well has to do with being able to ride a horse really well. How can you fix the bad habit of using reins for balance instead of your body and legs? Start slowly with this drill. At a walk, drop both stirrups and just walk for a minute or two, then pick up your stirrups and walk for a minute or two. The first sensation you will notice is the "ah haaa moment" of feeling your feet in the stirrups for the first time and how good that feels. This is the start to recognizing how valuable your lower legs are to balancing yourself properly without the reins. See if you can get the horse to walk slow and fast without tightening up on your reins for balance. If you all of a sudden get jolted in doing this exercise, use your right hand to grab the saddle or breastplate strap for balance, but NOT the reins. Pay attention to how many times you grab the saddle…this is how many times your swing would have been affected by this habit that needs to be addressed. Keep practicing this drill until you can change speeds/gears without the help of your reins and remember…Rome was not built in a day either. What you will start to discover is the use of your legs to grip and your body and butt to provide balance instead of your hands. When you feel like you mastered the walk drill, try it at a trot in small controlled increments building your self-confidence to be able to stay in the middle. And yes, your legs may be sore after this drill if you've never tried it before. Say hello to the new muscles you didn't know you needed to play polo and ride well.

Polo Pony Fitness

Key concepts to keep in mind: The task of getting horses fit for polo and being able to maintain their fitness during a polo season is a topic I love and have years of experience doing from 0-26 goal polo. Sometimes I succeeded in doing it extremely well and sometimes I did it with terrible mistakes that I had to learn the hard way, so listen close to what I found out! I have been responsible for preparing my own horses my entire career as far as dictating what the fitness and training program would be each day of the season. Therefore, I have a huge amount of notes to share with you about my experiences that may help you skip the absolute failures and focus on some proven techniques that can get you great results. There are some accepted norms in traditional polo pony fitness theories that I will share with you in this next section, but as far as a hard core rule of thumb to follow, the most common and proven steps to include are: polo ponies do best when you feed them well, give them plenty of time preparing in pre-season sets to build up strength and conditioning before moving to singles work, practice games, putting air in them and then tournament games. Those basic steps are the most common and widely used stages of fitness to follow when preparing your horses for polo.

Determining the best fitness plan for your individual horses depends on the type of player you are, the level of polo you will be playing, the type of horses you own and how long your season is that they will be in work. Yes you can run a successful program for a group of horses that is similar in most aspects for all of the horses and get to a decent result, but if you truly want to be a great polo player at any level of the sport, then you will want to start defining what will bring out each horse's natural abilities to peak performance. This means you will always be on the search for what you can add to the equation that will help them "each individually" be their absolute best.

There are so many variations in fitness routines depending on personal knowledge, so it would help to view the subject of polo pony fitness routines kind of like the idea behind group fitness classes for people at the gym vs using a personal trainer. You know, group classes where everyone does the same thing for an hour and the idea is to get in shape vs a personal trainer who is truly going to map out a plan for you individually to reach "your personal best and goals", the ones you define to them. Do you see my point? There is a huge difference in results you can attain depending on what level of detail you are willing to give to it. Always remember, each horse is like a person in that they are unique, so if you really want to get it right, figure out what you can add to the basic routine that brings out the best in each horse.

The topic of polo pony fitness truly needs its own book as I could talk about it all day long. So what I will attempt to do in the next section is summarize the absolute key ingredients and concepts your program should include at minimum. I truly believe being a great polo player is about having great horses underneath you and taking care of the fitness element is of utmost importance to get right.

Polo horses can be done in groups with an overall theory and just like the group fitness class idea, you will get some kind of results if you are consistent. But will you really get peak performance from everyone in every area of their abilities... maybe not. Here's another example of why it's so important to dial in to your specific needs as a player and the type of horses you own that you will be creating the plan for. For people trying to get in shape who are serious about their results: does a spin class produce the same fitness result as a cross fit class vs. an MMA fighter going through a conditioning camp vs. jogging? Do you see my point? The word "fitness" is a huge ocean of options as to what kind and level of fitness you are aiming for. Are you aiming for stamina, strength, conditioning, flexibility, endurance, low goal polo, high goal polo, green horse polo... these are the questions to ask when you are determining what your exercise routine and overall fitness plan should include. After you determine what type of polo you are preparing them for,

111

then decide what you want as your end result and create a plan to get there incorporating the five key ingredients to a great fitness program that I will describe in a minute.

Always keep these additional facts in mind regarding polo pony fitness. Getting the horses fit is one element to the plan and maintaining fitness and peak performance during the season, especially if it is a long one, are additional very important elements that should be included in your overall plan. Each step up in the level of polo player you are and the level of polo you are playing requires an additional level of fitness for these reasons. You are now going more places on the field and probably playing more often, which are both more demanding on the horse physically.

The right answer in knowing if the plan you are executing is right for you and your ponies is determined by how healthy and sound they are and how are they playing for you.

The five key ingredients to a great fitness program:
Here are the key ingredients I have found to produce successful results in a polo pony fitness program for any level of polo.

- ❖ Quality feed
- ❖ Consistent feeding times 7 days a week
- ❖ Daily exercise routine that suits your level of polo
- ❖ Your feed program should match the amount of exercise you plan on giving them
- ❖ You...paying attention to your horses and the 5 basic results indicators (health, overall condition, soundness, playing performance, attitude)

ONE: Quality feed. That of course sounds ridiculous as most people don't go to the feed store and ask for the crappy feed please, but you would be surprised just how many horses have no chance to be the true athlete they are because of the feed they are being given. You have to remember, your horses cannot get in the truck and go to the supermarket and get what they know they need...they rely on you to have it ready each day. It is your job as a horse owner to learn what feed works for the type of horses you have chosen to own. It is your duty as a horse owner to get educated on this topic, or be able to hire a groom who is educated and qualified to take care of this element. Most horsemen recognize that this is a lifelong process of rediscovery based on your own journey in horse ownership, knowledge and levels of polo that you will play. So always stay open minded to learning more on the topic of feed. It's important to pay close attention to the amounts of protein and fat in grains and the ratio of one to the other. Pay close attention to the protein content in the type of hay you choose as well and be especially aware that not all hay produces the same results. By educating yourself with these kinds of details as to the quality of content, you will now have some variables to work with in pursuit of creating the right formula for you personally. It is also important to find the right combination of grain with what type of hay that works well for the level of performance you are asking from the horses. Having the right combo in grain and hay can mean the difference of having really lean mean fighting machines vs heavy slow footed injury prone horses or worst case scenario underfed horses that are physically and mentally drained and unable to stay healthy. Quality feed in the right combination will provide a horse with superior agility and a well to draw from.

When I say quality feed, I also mean pay attention to the actual quality of the product visually, both grain and hay. Be on the lookout for changes in the horses as well as changes in the feed physically when you look at it. These details will help you be on the lookout for your best feed plan overtime.

TWO: **The importance of consistency.** One of the biggest favors you can do for your horses is to be consistent with your feed and the timing of it. Remember, if you keep your horses in stalls they have zero access to an open frig or a pasture to graze in. A horse's natural environment is out in the field grazing at all times of the day at its own discretion. To box them up and then be random in the timing or type of food that is delivered can be one of the worst things you can do to a horse. Not only does he not know when he is going to get to eat and starts tearing the barn down in his behavior to let you know, but his stomach will constantly be upset trying to adjust to the changing meal plan. One great gift you can give yourself and your string is to get educated on the best types of grain and hay for your horses' particular needs and then stick to it on a regular basis. And do not make the mistake to think that if you feed a horse at random times and are always changing feeds that you will achieve great results physically and your horse will remain healthy. You will spend a lot of vet bills figuring this small lesson out the hard way and your horses are the ones who will suffer from your mistakes. They will tell you immediately when your meal plan needs looking at by having an upset stomach, colic or diarrhea. Most people don't think it's a big deal to feed at changing times each day and feel as long as the horse ate they are achieving the same results. This is one of the largest and most dangerous mistakes to watch out for, because a horse can only handle so much change in their stomachs. If you are focused on the human element first and when the human is available because of work or the groom's day off...you need to adjust your focus to when the horse needs to eat and make plans to get there or have somebody there to deliver what they need to keep things consistent for the horse. That can be one of the most deadly mistakes, because you are just asking for your horse to colic, yet the most simple to avoid.

Consistency is a key factor in overall good horse management and that includes being consistent in feeding times, content of feed, daily exercise routine, time of day for the exercise routine and practice game schedule preparing the horses. When it comes to successful polo horse programs you will find one common denominator in all of them...consistency. By making an effort to be consistent with your feed content, feed times and a consistent exercise program to match, you will be on your way to a successful plan for your horses. If you are going to attempt to change one habit in your thought pattern for your personal horse plan after reading this book, I suggest you take the word consistency into deep consideration as the one to implement in all areas.

THREE: **Daily exercise routine that suits your level of polo and individual player needs.** Exercise routines are like weight loss magazine covers; everyone has a theory so be prepared to know that up front. The best proof of what works is the results that will show in the horse's appearance, health and performance on the field, case closed. Determining the best exercise routine for your horses depends on the type of player you are and the level of polo that you will be playing and here's why. Let's say you are a player who loves speed and at all chances you are racing around the field to try to make every play versus a person who has just started and is timid everywhere and therefore does not get much out of a hand canter. See what I mean…these are two different fitness needs.

The overall plan you use for your personal horses needs to suit the type of player you are, the level of polo you are playing and needs to incorporate an appropriate feed for the type of intensity level you require as the rider. This exercise routine should occur on a daily basis and be kept as consistently as possible as far as times it is done and days of the week, so the horses can have the best results.

One of the most important factors to always think about before and during the season in making your overall daily fitness routine is to always remember each horse is unique. Each one has its own set of thoughts, its own set of old injuries, its own tolerance level, its own sensitivities and its own physical attributes or lack of. There will always be a basically similar regimen you can follow with the group as a whole to get them into shape and maintain them during the season, but if you really

117

want to get all of what a horse has to offer than you will do yourself a large favor by keeping an open mind if one is not performing as well as the others. They may need to have some adjustments made in the feed or the exercise regimen to reach their peak performance. Be on the lookout for these clues.

FOUR: **Your feed program should match the amount of exercise you plan on giving them**. Note to self...let's start at the beginning. A good feed program for your horses should be kept up all year long including off-season when turned out. A good feed program for your string or polo pony during the polo season, especially if they have not been receiving or off of grain for a while, begins pre-season with the introduction of grain at a tolerance level they can utilize for the work load they are doing and increasing the amount of grain as you increase the workload. That is the basic formula that will ensure the best results.

If you over feed horses and do not give them a proportionate and consistent amount of exercise to utilize the feed you are putting in them, you will be building a bomb in many ways both physically and mentally. This can be deadly for a horse. So always make sure the feed you are putting in them matches the exercise plan. You can also do a lot of physical damage to a horse by under feeding it or feeding it with low quality hay and grain that it either cannot digest well or does not provide the necessary nutrients in the right proportion for the physical demand you are attempting to get it ready for. This is why it is extremely important to match the food with the level of athlete you are looking to manage.

If you have some horses that start the season really skinny you can add extra feed to them by giving an additionally "small" portion of grain at lunchtime to spread the intake out over the day, versus trying to force feed a huge bucket of grain into them once or twice a day. This method can also be used to help a horse who is lacking catch up to the others, or one who eats really slow or is fallen a little weak during the season to catch up to its full potential. Always remember that a horse's natural make up is to be out walking the countryside grazing at will, which means their natural way of eating is all day long. So you can see where this method of increasing feed may be a safer way to introduce additional food and have a better overall effect both safely and effectively, as it goes in line with the horse's natural make up.

FIVE: You, paying attention to your horses and the 5 basic results indicators. Now comes the real work...you. It is your responsibility as a polo player and horse owner to know the proper way to care for your horses, as this is your partner on the field. One fact, is that each player has a different level of participation with the actual behind the scenes day to day business of taking care of the ponies, but whichever way you slice it, the player and horse owner needs to take full responsibility for these great athletes by learning the right way to care for them or being able to hire a professional groom or barn manager who does know how to take care of them. Be diligent about reminding yourself to take into serious consideration the **5 basic results indicators: health, overall condition, soundness, playing performance, attitude.** When you make a point to start incorporating these thoughts during the entire polo season, including pre-season when you are in the process of legging them up and daily during the playing season, you are setting yourself up for the greatest chance at a successful season with your horse management. Be ready to make adjustments to your program if you find that any of your results indicators are telling you there is an issue with a particular horse or the entire group. This is the way you become a better horseman and in turn a better polo player. Being a better polo player has a lot to do with the quality of your horse program and in being open to learning what works and what doesn't. Don't let your personal ego stop you from taking a hard look at your results indicators, they are the proof that what you are doing is working or failing in your personal horse program.

Learn how to assess your fitness program results. Horses will speak to you directly through their behaviors and appearance, so always pay attention to the 5 basic results indicators of the job you are doing no matter what the specific details. They will help you determine your strengths and where you are having weaknesses in your program and what needs to be addressed to get your barn and string in tip top shape. As the polo player you should be aware and educated about these things even if you have a groom who you have hired to handle the horses. Learning this kind of information is how you become a better polo player over time. Additionally, you will be able to discuss with your groom or barn manager how you think things are going and actually be able to chime in on where you see some room for improvement. What I will explain below is the insider information on how to improve your string by knowing how to measure your success or failure. These are the things to be on the lookout for in knowing when to make adjustments in your program. And remember I said this: when you find something that works well…stick to it!

5 basic fitness program results indicators

- ❖ **Health**
- ❖ **Overall condition**
- ❖ **Soundness**
- ❖ **Playing performance**
- ❖ **Attitude**

All of these factors can indicate how your program is going, so be on the lookout for changes in any one or more of these mentioned above. If you notice one of them being an issue, then start looking into the cause until you get it fixed and headed in the right direction. If you notice your entire string has an issue in one or more areas, then you should recognize there is something "you" as program director needs to adjust so that the entire string can reach its full potential during the season. For example, if you are having a certain leg injury that keeps occurring in multiple horses, start asking questions like a detective until you find the source. Is it the footing on the track, is it the exercise program lacking a solid foundation preseason, is it the way the horses are being bandaged, is it that you gave the horses no foundation of strength in conditioning at speed before tournament games...these are the kinds of questions to start asking until you find the source...then fix it. Apply the same concept in investigative questions if you have a common health issue among several horses such as tying up or colicing until you determine the source...then make a plan to implement a change until you extinguish the health issue that keeps reoccurring. There is always a common denominator in trouble, so start looking for it to answer your personal situation This is the continual process to apply that will bring out the best horseman in you and the best results in a successful horse management program. If you keep at it long enough, you will eventually discover a program that works well for your specific needs and will give you confidence with your horses.

How Your Horsemanship affects your Polo

What is horsemanship? Horsemanship is the connection between the human and equine athlete and it is everything to being the absolute best in the sport of polo as a player no matter what your handicap. No matter what your current level of polo, horsemanship and your attention to it is where you will find the greatest satisfaction and passion. It is also where you will find and create your largest secret weapon on the polo field. This connection will make you feel invincible and undeniably proud when done right. It is also the first and loudest most obvious missing factor to be noticed in average players.

The term horsemanship encompasses everything about how you are able to interact and care for your equine partner and goes way beyond the ability to ride or know certain horsey terminology. Horsemanship is an art that goes back for centuries, as horses have been used throughout history to conquer some of the greatest walls of impossibility. It is through the horse's willingness to give their heart and souls to the human being that mankind has been able to bring history forward where the task seemed impossible. Polo is no different, as it is the horse that elevates the game to its highest levels of beauty and passion. It is the connection of great horseman and horse that drives every polo player to do more and be more. Horsemanship is the edge that is invisible to the naked eye or first time viewer of the sport, but to a seasoned professional or fan, this is the ultimate connection to witness and be inspired by.

Why is horsemanship so important to you as a polo player? The reason is this: horses are what can provide you with the extra edge over other players...always. Horsemanship is the blueprint to putting it all together with your horses. Good horsemanship in a polo player is what will bring out a horse's best ability to turn quicker for the play, to out run the competition, to make up yards for a dumb mistake and to out-handle your opponent in one on one situations. No matter how strong you are or how many bridle combinations you think you can come up with to man handle a horse around the field, the ultimate moments of excellence are when the horse is actually "wanting" to think with you and attempts to dig as deep as possible physically for you. This is why good horsemanship is important. Imagine if you could have that kind of an advantage over your opponent? To have this kind of an advantage is the key to unlock the vault of success. Without good horsemanship, you are seriously limiting your potential as a polo player.

It is also a life-long endeavor and amazing journey for those of you who love horses. If your plan to become a great polo player before reading this book, was to become a great ball striker, learn strategy and that would get you somewhere in the sport, I got news for you. You not only need a horse, you need the horse to be "on your side" in the battle if you really want to make your mark as a player. Horses will speak to you directly through their actions, appearance and performance so always pay attention to what you feel, see and are witnessing when it comes to those three details as they are huge clues to what's going on with your horses.

In my opinion the definition of a true horseman is so complex, but in its greatest form, to me the greatest compliment and stamp of a true horseman is this statement... the sum of who you are to the horse. A real horseman is well respected by the horse and will do anything the person asks because of the level of respect they have earned from the horse. This invisible trust and faith is the sign of a true horseman and trust me when I say, horses are well aware of who's who in the bunch of humans they come in contact with. Make no mistake, a horse will take notes on its rider and they do have a memory.

A true horseman knows that the next new horse will always bring something new to your library of knowledge, no matter how many years are spent in the barn. If you're wondering if you have achieved some level of accomplishment in the department of horsemanship so far as a player, just ask yourself this question. Have you outgrown the horse you started playing polo on yet? How did you know you were ready to move to the next level of horse? When did you become aware that a horse had more to give? Was it a certain horse that made you aware of this feeling that you could have a deeper connection and do more? This is your personal horsemanship in progress and yes, everyone is capable of growing its potential throughout your career as a polo player. This is the largest and most powerful secret weapon in your arsenal as a polo player, so get to work.

When a horse agrees with your participation they will give you all they have within them and this is why as a polo player you need to approach this subject as the most important class to get an A in...so keep studying ☺.

CHAPTER SEVEN

Your Handicap...

Strategies for improving your handicap

With an organized plan of attack, you will give yourself the greatest chance of improvement in your abilities as a polo player. With each new skill you are able to master, you will be giving yourself new opportunities on the field that didn't look like options before. These new opportunities and risks you will be willing to try, will lead you into the next dimension of truly understanding the game and being able to become a functioning part of a team. Having the ability to be a functioning part of a team, even if the players change is how you become an accomplished polo player. If improving your handicap is a goal of yours, here are some strategies of how to go about it in the day-to-day fun and adrenaline rush of playing polo. It is so easy to get caught up in the rush of details and excitement of it all, that you sometimes lose sight of some really key elements that can help you improve your actual handicap if that's a goal of yours. So these are some things to always keep in mind, that over time will eventually pull you forward to solid improvement, no matter what level of polo you play.

Determine your ultimate goal for yourself. Once you know your destination, you can then get to work on the details. Your personal goal might be a certain handicap, it might be a certain tournament win, or it might be to just be able to stay on the horse if you just started. Whatever is your goal at this point...define it. As you go, you may want to re ask yourself that question every so often, because your goals may change as you get farther into the sport. It is very easy to get lost in the details and forget what you wanted for yourself, so be open to reminding yourself every so often.

Go to Practice with an organized plan of attack. This will help you make improvements in the segments of your game that are troubling you or holding you back. Without a plan of attack how to address things that challenge you in games, you are just logging hours reacting when you play practice games. To truly understand how to execute proper set play logic and play properly at your position with a team can propel you into the next level of your game without doubt. So make a point to always have a plan of what each practice game is for personally, so you can get the most out of it for you and your horses.

Play Tournament games…lots of them. Tournament games provide a place to be under pressure and pushed from all angles to perform. It is in a tournament game that everything from horse preparation, to penalty shooting, understanding of set plays and execution, learning finesse under pressure, to ball striking…everything is tested. It takes this kind of pressure to force you to make moves and think through things you wouldn't be pressured to do within the comfort of practice games, that you can engage in at will or just canter around and have a good time in. When you have no pressure to be challenged, you have no need to grow.

Play at multiple clubs against different players. This will give you the experience of coming up against the unknown in new players and having to rely on your skills to navigate the field of players, as opposed to a pecking order of the usual suspects in a single club playing experience. When you only play at one club, you may become stagnant or plateau because you are only challenged by the top players at your club and may actually be less likely to engage in attempting to challenge yourself against them due to respect for the local pecking order you have become comfortable within. Other clubs will have various types of players and each new player you come up against will challenge your abilities and will open your eyes to different styles of play, which will ultimately broaden your viewpoint on possibilities and the need for improvement.

Find who or what inspires you. Study the best players at the top of the sport or the ones around you that inspire you in how they play. Use these people as examples for what interests you to learn: their playing style, their hitting or riding style, their horses or even certain moves that they are able to pull off. Study the part that impresses you about them and how they make it happen. When you look for inspiration above your ability, you will become curious. This curiosity will challenge you to learn more for yourself. Start watching players you are inspired by and see what you find.

Always play with mallets that give you confidence. Having mallets you are confident in, especially when it is time to hit the tournament field, is a tremendous asset to a player and gives you that extra edge. Always have mallets that suit your individual needs and give you the results you are looking for. It is like a world-class surgeon going into the operating room with a dull scalpel. It doesn't matter how brilliant a surgeon, the equipment will have an effect on the outcome of the task at hand.

Stick n ball, lots of quality stick n ball. When you give time to quality stick n ball, you are giving time to improving one of your most important tools as a player and that is being able to execute shots with accuracy and finish goals. Being a good ball striker is always beneficial in every aspect of the game, but being an "excellent" ball striker will open amazing opportunities within your game and as a potential team mate in demand, which will lead to better polo. When you stick n ball, actually take the time to practice making goals by setting up targets to shoot at. Make sure to hit penalty shots as well as shots at a make shift goal from all angles to simulate a game experience. Spend some of your stick n ball time each session putting pressure on yourself to execute certain shots you have predetermined. Giving yourself this kind of practice will build a new level of confidence when you hit the field for the game.

Pay attention to how you are mounted. How you are mounted and horse management are the most important factors to truly improving your handicap at any level. Whether you own the horses or are playing borrowed or rented horses, it is important to realize as a player you can only do what the quality of your horses allow you to do on the field. When you have the advantage of good horses that are well fed, trained and physically fit to handle the needs of your polo and are suitable for your level of polo, you will have the best chance of having a great personal game performance. So pay close attention to what you are riding at all times and especially in tournament games. Having the right horses in your string will define you as a player and provide you the opportunity to reach your highest handicap potential. If you are an aspiring professional looking to move up the ranks, you need to have this topic as priority #1, as most jobs are won and lost over the horse factor.

Have polo ponies in your string that are suitable for you personally. This concept is everything to a good polo player and may need to be adjusted as you progress, as to the style of horse that best suits your needs. Always be realistic as to what kind of horse best suits you personally and what horses you feel most confident on. Remember, it is your personal confidence that will allow you to push your limits and that comes when you are riding horses that suit you. Those are the chukkers you will play your best polo.

Make solid horse purchases. Make sure to purchase horses that suit your needs and give you the most confidence. Remember, confidence leads to a player's best game performances. So the more horses you have in your string that give you confidence, the more chances of great chukkers you will have. Make buying horses about adding to or upgrading your benchmark group of horses at the top of your string and you will be on your way to buying horses that will be in your string for a long time. Let me make it really clear how much of a disadvantage you give yourself riding or buying the wrong horses or ones that are not prepared properly. For those of you that follow auto racing, if champion Nascar driver Jimmy Johnson entered the Daytona 500 in a minivan with limited fuel and a few low tires, how good do you think he could do...even with his champion skills? Good luck buddy, wear a helmet it's going to be a long day!

Always be looking for ways to improve your string. The key to consistent improvement is the quality of horses you have the ability to play. Always be on the lookout for how you can improve your horses with the program you have in place or the adjustments you can make to it that will bring out the best in each horse that you own. Polo horse ownership means you will always be presented with scenarios to solve in playing capabilities and soundness preservation. So, if you are going to be

135

diligent in one area and horses interest you, invest every bit of attention to how you can improve each horse individually and you will be amazed at how much it does to your overall performance on the field. This may mean be more selective in your purchases, it may mean start to evaluate your horse fitness program for holes, it may mean start to evaluate your feeding program to see if its providing you with the right amount of power or longevity in competition, it may mean evaluating your training program pre-season to see if it's really getting your horses to their full potential or it may mean to start evaluating your horses bridles they play in to see if they are using what is appropriate for the type of horse and player you are at this point in your skill level. No matter what the detail you choose to start with, if you make an attempt to always be looking for what can improve your string, you will have the best chance at gaining the extra edge to becoming the best polo player possible at any handicap.

Always keep your mind open to learning more. This is the absolute most valuable gift you can give yourself as a player who wants to improve. Put your ego aside and always be open to this thought. What you know today will evolve as you become more experienced and have the opportunity to play more tournament polo and especially when paired up against higher rated players than yourself.

There is always something more to be learned and no matter how much polo you have played, you will always find new details on the same subjects and strategies. So keep your mind open to learning and especially in the horse and strategy departments, they are huge libraries of information to absorb over time.

Do your homework behind the scenes and between games. This means all of the work, including back at the barn, how to improve your string, on the stick n ball field in your hitting mistakes, finding your personal strategy mistakes, your horse line up mistakes, your pregame warm up mistakes, your horse fitness or schooling mistakes, your shots on goal mistakes...look for all of them and then go to work. Your homework is to find your mistakes from the last game and attempt to solve them, so that you can remove that element that was holding you back from having your best performance. Even if you only discover one mistake or improvement you would like to make from each game, just go to work on how to improve that single topic for the next game. The time in between games behind the scenes is where the real work to being a good polo player is done. This type of work is what makes a great player great. Make sure to put special attention to your horses so they are ready for the next game especially in addressing any soundness, feeding or fitness issues. If you will make a habit of giving all of these basic topics or even just one that you've singled out listed above some attention during the period between each game, you will be on the road to sure success in improving yourself as a polo player. If this is the first time you are hearing or reading about these basic details, I suggest you reread this small section a few times until it becomes second nature to repeat it. This is the foundation of gradual and steady success at any level of the sport whether you are an amateur or an aspiring professional or a weekend recreational player. The work you put in behind the scenes is where you plant the seeds to your greatest success as a player.

Determine if you are making the 3 most common mistakes in polo that hold people back...then quit doing them ASAP!

ONE: Stop watching the ball. Say what????...oh yes, that's exactly what I said. One of the biggest errors in most players that can cause the most damage on a polo field is the bad habit of watching the polo ball. Yes, watching the polo ball...is BAD. Why is it bad? When you are focused on the polo ball you will be late to the play 100% of the time, because the ball is only secondary to the person who is hitting it or the play that is developing. If you think about it like this you will always give yourself better timing and actually arrive at the play much quicker. Have you ever watched a border collie waiting for someone to throw a ball? Yeah, that's what you look like with no awareness of what's going on around you. Also, when you are focused on a ball your focus is down on the ground, when it should be up on a player or the position you need to be in. The ball will always come and arrive in the next destination according to the play that is developing, so it is necessary to start learning to read plays to know where the ball will be. If you are watching the ball to know the answer, I guarantee you, you will be late to the play. Or even worse, watching the ball will almost always cause you to commit fouls. Feel like you are late to some plays, but not sure you are having this problem? Dare ya to get one of your games videoed, then get some popcorn and a remote and watch the game. When you watch the video, look at one element. Where is your head focused during the game?

139

Watching the ball will help you commit some amazing fouls, because your attention is focused on the wrong thing. This is an easy habit to break, once you realize how late you are and the amount of fouls you are committing because of this one simple issue. So go ahead and take a look at your videos. But I warn ya now...you might be surprised what you find ☺.

TWO: **Stop riding parallel to the play**. This has to be one of the most frustrating mistakes a player can make that is usually the mystery cause responsible for many fouls you can't figure out. The reason the mystery fouls happen, is because you are always entering the flow of the play and traffic from a 90-degree angle when you do engage. It is a very common mistake, but an easy one to fix. Anytime you catch yourself riding parallel to the pack of players and the flow of the play, immediately adjust your horse's speed to fall in line with the pack...like a trail ride, one behind the other. Take a moment to look behind you to make sure of the speed of traffic before entering (just like merging on a freeway in your car)...and then don't hesitate, make yourself adjust immediately. When you catch yourself doing this mistake, should you drop back or go forward you ask? Here is the question to ask yourself that will determine your answer and this is a safe default in most situations. Count the players ahead of you. If you see there are two opponents ahead and only one of your teammates, then move ahead to the closest opponent so you can help your teammate out. If there are two of your teammates already up ahead with two

140

opponents, then drop behind them to the next open opponent.

You get the idea, just look ahead and count the players. Then assess the scene and make a move immediately to the spot that looks like there is a free opponent. This simple move will put you back in the flow of the game and the rest will develop from there. But nothing can happen until you get in the correct position where the flow of the plays will be happening and that is either in front of or behind the hitter…not to the side of the pack. Traveling parallel to the pack of players and flow of play is not the place to be the playmaker. Make this one adjustment to your game and watch how much starts to make sense in areas that completely confused you before.

THREE: **Stop hesitating, make a choice and go for it!** This has to be one of the absolute most common mistakes that holds so many people back from being as good as they could be. Doubt…everyone has it no matter how long you have been playing. You know, that moment that feels like forever when you see a play developing and you're not sure what is the right play for you to make…should I go or wait for the next play? The mistake holds you back because of the amount of yards you are galloping and losing with this thought running through your mind…should I do it or will I make a mistake? When you allow yourself to have that thought as you run down the field, you are not actually getting anything accomplished, except putting miles on your horse. The longer you stay in self-doubt and questioning, the longer the amount of time you are giving your opponent to stage an even worse attack that you will be way too late to do anything substantial about by the time you pull the trigger on your decision. That is, if you ever actually make a decision. Best way to break a bad or unproductive habit or thought is to replace it with a healthy one that can help the situation at hand. Here is your new thought to replace the old one that will help you make a move instead of wasting yards galloping in indecision. "Who has possession of the ball right now, my team or the other team?" Answering this question to yourself as your default counselor, each time the situation presents itself, will lead you to two immediate options for a solution. By choosing one of these new options and getting to work, you will set yourself in motion in a productive direction to get something done and out of doubt. The answers to the question and their solutions respectively are as follows.

Situation #1: If my team has the ball, then my solution is that I need to get in line to hit or receive the ball as quickly as possible...therefore, I will move immediately to be in the right spot for that to be able to happen.

Situation #2: If the other team has the ball, then my immediate solution is that I need to get to the closest opponent and take them out in defense for my team.

Use these new choices, as your default tools to help you make a solid decision when doubt creeps in. Please note, there are always more complex reasons to make additional moves on top of the basic decision, but having these as your "basic default decisions" to always fall back on will set everything back in motion to actually pull the trigger on making a move.

Learn how to overcome a plateau before it becomes permanent. When you find yourself in this situation, it is time to go back and redefine your goal to yourself at this point in your polo career and journey. You may have lost sight of it all together or it got lost in the adrenaline rush that goes on in the daily details. Or, you may have already achieved your original goal and hadn't set a new one to move forward to. This is a common situation and one that is very easy to fix. You can overcome this by mentally redefining your goal for yourself at this point and then go to work on it from this day forward. A new goal can even be a singular skill you want to achieve as opposed to a monumental statement or title. What the goal is, only needs to inspire you. This small habit will re-open your ability to improve at any stage of the game. The new goal is what will reignite inspiration, curiosity, purposeful stick n ball, riding or practice efforts and those efforts are what will step you right past the plateau you have been stuck in.

143

CHAPTER EIGHT

Polo Mallets...

Determine the best mallet for your individual needs.

When choosing your mallets it is important to determine what is comfortable to you and yes, uniquely you. Many people own mallets and have no idea what the theory is in the style of mallet they are using and trust me, this is more common than you can imagine and here is why. Most people starting out in polo just buy what they are told to buy or have read that sounds right, or they went into a shop with their pro and the pro told them what to use. None of how you get your first set of mallets is wrong, they will all get you off and running, but over time it is important to start identifying which mallets feel great in your hands and which ones are causing arm injuries and doubt. Start paying attention to which mallets make you feel really confident and which ones feel awkward in your hand. Awkwardness is normal when you first start, but over time when you stick n ball and or practice, there will be certain mallets that you naturally gravitate to. Start paying attention to their similarities, this is the start to the unique style that works for you. Mallets are all hand made so there are many options in cane thickness, stiffness or flexibility, mallet head weights, mallet head sizes and shapes, handle and grip sizes and thickness etc. All of these things can be customized and you may not even realize there are that many options, but there are. One of my favorite things is going through a fresh batch of canes and placing heads on the ones I want to try and determining if it's a good 52,52 ½ or 53…hundreds of canes…totally fun afternoon spent in the mallet shop. For example, my mallets have been custom made through most of my career by Nano's Polo Mallets. Owners Nano and Irene Perez have the market cornered on customer service and completely understanding how important it is to get things right for a polo player when it comes to their mallets. For example, we went the ultimate distance in customization by creating a 52 1/2'" mallet…my absolute favorite size! Yes, size matters and they are saints for their attention to details! Why a 52 ½" you ask??? Confidence. There just seems to be that huge mental leap from the 52" horse to the 53" horse…sounds funny, but when you think of a 53 you think of a monster size horse and a flagpole for the stick. Mentally it's all in how you draw confidence from what you pick up and this is an extreme example, but will hit home with the point I am trying to make. It is important for a polo player to use what gives them the most confidence. This will be the mallet that you hit the best with consistently, no matter how beat up it is and is always your go to weapon. These are the mallets you want more of, so go to work on finding them.

The most common question asked about mallets: Does using a heavier or stiffer mallet mean I will hit farther? Most people think that if you use a heavier mallet you will automatically hit the ball farther, but it's not always true. Obviously there is some math behind a heavier mallet doing more damage than a light one. But if you don't know how to use it properly you will not only wear your arm out, you may create an unnecessary tennis elbow from trying to wield that heavy broomstick when turning the ball and the aftershock vibration of hitting over time. What will make you hit the ball farther is the proper technique and the proper balance of the right mallet. Once you understand the proper technique you can start playing with mallet weights, but pay attention to where the extra weight is coming from. Is it in the thickness of the cane or is it in the weight of the head or is it a balanced combo? It really makes a difference to determine where the extra weight is coming from and how dense is the head you have on the cane. For example here are some details that will affect the overall weight of a mallet when it comes to the head: a very dense heavy head, a large size head but a light overall weight, a soft or "green uncured" head that absorbs more shock than it delivers or a completely dew frayed mallet head. All of those examples are factors that will potentially affect overall mallet weight and functional performance capabilities. So when it comes to hitting well and getting the most distance, that is why it is so important to start

149

paying attention to the small details that add to a mallet's make up in overall weight and functionality. As you progress in knowledge about your mallets, keep in mind which mallets you really do hit the ball well with and start basing your new purchases off of those. Here are some new options to try and experiment with as you go: heavier heads, different style canes and maybe a few thoughts toward the grip size and dimensions. My point, the right mallet and knowing how to use it is more valuable than a mallet just because it is heavier.

Keep an eye out for potential problems with your mallets: What does it mean when my mallets are wrung and how do I check them for potential issues? When a mallet has been used a while some can become what is called "wrung", which means that the head is no longer stationary when you strike the ball. A wrung mallet may not be visibly obvious to the untrained eye, but for the user it will give you the sensation of unexplained shanked balls and a sharp or minor decline in your accuracy depending on how wrung it is. The way to check if a mallet is wrung is to hold the grip of the mallet tightly with one hand and grab the mallet head with the other hand. Attempt to turn or twist the head, does it move at all? Or does it stay completely in place with no give? A mallet's head should not move at all when you attempt this rotation. If it moves, that means you need to give it to the repair shop or person who fixes your mallets, because the cane has been damaged at the base where it is taped right next to the head. This is usually hard to see because the point of the break or crack is covered by tape and paint. The other way to check if your mallets are wrung is to place the head on the ground and hold the grip in your hand. Place one foot on the mallet head and attempt with your hand to twist the grip. If you are able to twist the grip in any direction, it is probably time to send this mallet to the repairman. The good news is this; you may have just solved some of your accuracy when hitting issues…maybe.

Why do people tape their mallet heads and what is the best way to do it? Taping mallet heads is done for a couple of reasons. One main reason is to prevent fraying of the wood when you stick n ball or play on a wet or dew covered field. The moisture of a wet field will eventually over time start to eat away the strike zone of your mallet head. It will look like someone took a shredder to your nice varnished or painted head that you started with. It also affects the overall weight of the mallet head when that happens, as a portion of its overall weight has now been eaten up. When this happens you may notice your shots do not have that crisp solid power when you hit. They will feel mushy or light when you make impact with the ball.

The way to prevent this deterioration from happening is to tape your mallet heads with electrical or duct tape and here is how you do it. Get a roll of electrical tape and start at one end of the mallet head, about an inch or two from the end and begin to circle the head with the tape. Cross over the center and onto the other end of the head, stopping at about an inch or two from the end. When you hit the end, head back the other direction repeating the circling of tape until you are back where you started. Taping your mallet heads will help you preserve the mallet heads for a longer life span. By taping the head with either a wide strip of duct tape trimmed to fit on each side of the head or by rounding the head with electrical tape, you will also add a slight bit of head weight, which is always good as well.

The importance of good mallets and the confidence they bring. Having confidence in your mallets is like wearing the right size shoes. You know when you have exactly the right ones and you don't have to think about it...they're just there doing their job and they feel good. A mallet is very similar, in that when you are using the right one you don't even think about it. Having confidence in whatever piece of equipment you are using means you can focus on the task at hand of being a better polo player, anything less takes up some of your concentration that you could be focusing on the game with. Especially important to point out is the attention you spend thinking about a certain shot you do not want to try because it hurts your arm. Could it be that you are using the wrong mallet and it is taking from your confidence, because of how uncomfortable or painful it is? Having mallets you are confident in is a great feeling, especially when it is time to hit the tournament field. The feeling you get when you lay them out is an extra moment of "let's get this started" and especially that go to favorite. It just gives you that extra edge.

Ps…still wondering about that 52 ½" ???
ask Nano and Irene…www.polomallets.com

CHAPTER NINE

Polo Tips...

Tips for the new polo player, the amateur, the aspiring professional

Polo is one of the greatest sports you will ever play and requires a lot of moving parts to function well together, to be the best. You will do your personal best if you recognize that each level of polo requires a larger input of participation mentally and physically. This is why no matter how many games you play, there is always that detail or details that leave a question to solve in your mind. You know, that drive home from the game where you find your mind racing about horses, your strategy, your fouls, something that happened in the game, your actual skills, playing internationally to meet people who share the same passion...there is always the curiosity that calls out to know more. It is this curiosity that leads to the discovery of a well of passion that every true polo player has touched and felt the power of. This is what has kept the sport of polo around for over 2,000 years and is still alive today. No matter what level of polo you choose to play or what capacity you choose to do it in, there is a tremendous amount of information that will help you along the way to having the greatest experience possible if you are willing to look for it.

This chapter is about those absolute key points that I feel are important to give some thought to as you go. I broke it down into three sections of important tips to keep in mind, so that you can just go directly to what applies to what you are looking for or curious about. There are a million more tips to include, but this should get you started on the absolute basics.

Tips for players who are new to polo

Here are some things to keep in mind as you start in polo. The most important factor to remember when starting the sport of Polo is to take it at a pace that is manageable for safety, fun and staying within your budget. Polo is extremely addictive and the best kind of addiction to have and warning…it is incurable☺! This advice will help you get started and on your way to one of the greatest sports you will ever play.

❖ Learn to ride first, spend as much time as you can in the saddle until you feel completely confident and safe with the horse. If you have the ability to take additional riding lessons, use all of what you have available to you to get as much time in the saddle learning about horses as possible. This will be the best personal investment of time you will make when you start. Learn how to be safe on and around horses and make sure you learn how to stop a horse properly. Knowing how to do this in the beginning will give you confidence know you can shut things down at any time, should you become uncomfortable with the situation.

❖ Buy a foot mallet and ball to practice with so you can start to get familiar with all the shots and always have a way to be practicing your swing and rotation even when you don't have access to horses. Might be a good idea to buy two so you can hit the ball back and forth with a friend and practice your accuracy in passing the ball. You can buy one at: www.polomallets.com

❖ Take plenty of lessons and give time to learning about the rules of the game before actually committing to play in your first game.

❖ Ride many horses before your first horse purchase to determine the style of horse that is right for you and the one that gives you the most confidence. Do not buy any horses until you are ready and confident that they are safe for you. Older horses with a lot of experience can be a great first purchase option.

❖ Watch as many games as you can to start learning about positions and plays on the field.

❖ Find an instructor that can teach you the proper techniques and foundation to hitting the polo ball correctly on both sides of the horse, offside and nearside. This will ensure quality stick n ball time going forward.

❖ To ensure a quality and valuable asset to your new habit, always keep this thought in mind. When you are ready to buy your first polo horse, make sure you can answer a clear and defined "yes" to the following two questions:

1) Do I feel safe on this horse?

2) Does this horse give me confidence when I ride and play him or her?

Tips for Amateur polo players

Here are some things to keep in mind to help you improve your skill level and handicap. Always be paying attention to the following topics, as they are the key ingredients in improving your abilities on the polo field. Improving your personal abilities on the polo field is what will increase your handicap over time.

- ❖ Do all you can to always be improving your string. Good horses are the key to being your best.

- ❖ If you can't afford to buy top made horses, then do the work to help the horses you can afford to buy, become the absolute best they can be.

- ❖ Spend time on the stick n ball field, working on goal shooting and all shots that are hard.

- ❖ Create a proper game day routine, so that you are in game mode when you hit the field.

❖ Learn how to take a man properly. This is the most important skill to master.

❖ Learn the concept of "man-line-ball" as your default counselor.

❖ Be ready to be honest with what you are missing in skills, get help defining it if necessary.

❖ Watch game videos of yourself playing and if possible with a professional for advice.

❖ Figure out the style of play you prefer and the position on a team that best suits your style of play. Once you determine what position that is, go to work on mastering the position in skills.

❖ As you advance in the sport you will learn many new techniques how to do the same tasks you have been doing since you started, only in a much more effective way. So always be open to learning new strategies that could help your game and abilities.

❖ If you are hiring pros, make sure to discuss with them what you would like to improve on and be specific. Remember, the pro "works for you".

❖ When hiring pros, be specific on defining who pays what expenses and what the timeline will be.

❖ When buying horses, always create a clear exit plan with the seller that dictates what happens if the horse does not work out for you, especially when purchasing horses and importing them.

Tips for the aspiring Professional

Being a professional polo player is one of the greatest occupations you could ever have, as it will literally be your passport to travel the world playing what I believe is the world's greatest game. You will also have the opportunity to meet some amazing people and horses on the journey. Be ready to do the work it will take behind the scenes to be prepared for your next game. Do not expect for any reason that it will be handed to you. At times there will be great people who will see your talent and want to help you achieve your goals, so always show respect and appreciation for those people along the way no matter how small their contribution. The road can sometimes be challenging, but the rewards are well worth it. When you do get the call from a 10 goal player or the highest rated professional at your club to play on their team, you will know you are doing it right. I have gotten that call many times and I can tell you there is no other feeling like it as an aspiring professional. I can also tell you that I reached a handicap of 5 goals, because of my work ethic off the field, my ability to listen, to be open minded and my attitude to give 100% on the field at all times...no excuses. So I can tell you with expert experience this advice...it is possible if you will just do the work. Always remember as a professional player aspiring to be the best at the top, unless you are at the 9 goal level and above…you are as good as your last game in people's minds. This is important to remember, because you are always very replaceable as a professional player and you will have a substantial investment at risk if you fail to recognize this fact.

Pay attention to the small details and do not party yourself out of the season, as the social scene during a polo season can be the largest drain for some of the greatest young professionals. Good luck with your professional career in polo and hopefully these tips will help you along the way to achieving your dream in the sport of polo. I know I have achieved mine and can tell you that this will be the most amazing journey you will ever take, so get ready for the adventure of a lifetime that you could never predict ☺.

❖ Build your string…it is everything. A good string is how you stand out above the rest of the players at your handicap.

❖ Learn to be an above average rider so you can jump on any horse and be able to perform.

❖ Pay close attention to the importance of practicing specifics. Be detailed about what you are working on in skills when you practice or stick n ball.

❖ Be open to being told what to do by the team captain. Always be respectful and open to listening...always.

❖ Learn the art of not biting under pressure...no matter what...stay focused on your performance.

❖ Always remember...attitude is everything. The right attitude will get you more jobs than talent.

❖ Get your game videos at every chance, so you can study them for mistakes and learn how to correct them.

❖ Find what challenges you and practice it until you figure it out. If you can't master it on your own, get help from a pro who "can do" what you are trying to achieve.

❖ Remember this fact: to become a top professional at any handicap you must play against better players that will challenge your skills. This is how you improve.

❖ Unless your handicap number is 10 goals, you still have things to learn. So get to work and drop the ego if you want to be great.

❖ When it comes to the question of selling the best horses in your string if an amazing financial offer comes up, you will need to make serious consideration to these thoughts. If you sell your best horses you will be limiting your abilities on the field to perform or move up in handicap. The money you will receive may be desperately needed, but take serious consideration what the loss of that chukker will do to your handicap and ability on the field before you say "yes" to selling your best horse.

❖ Sometimes jobs are won and lost on a pros horses or lack of. Always be aware of the message you are sending by the quality of your string and the care of them.

❖ Always make a point to take care of and recognize your grooms, they are the foundation of a solid team of success to both horses and top players.

❖ What will always sell you, as a professional is your performance on the polo field. So make a point to do your best job when you play, each and every time you get the opportunity.

❖ When you go to the field, be a professional in all aspects of your performance. Prepare yourself and your horses to the absolute best of your ability, as each time you go to the field you are your own advertisement...so make it a good one.

CHAPTER TEN

A summary note from Sunny ...

I hope you enjoyed reading this book and you have some new insights and strategies to use that will help bring out the best polo player in you, as well as help you understand things that just never made sense. Always remember, the horses are your legs in the game and they will take you everywhere you want to go. So do your best to take care of them and always respect their needs and the fact that they are the world's greatest athletes.

Some of the topics I covered in this first book truly deserve a book of their own and will be getting just that as the Let's Talk Polo book series is released. So please understand that the information included here, is what I feel are the absolute basics you need to know if you want to improve as a polo player. In other words, you better at least know these basics no matter what level of the game you are at. This information is what I would consider step one of building your personal rocket ship. If some of these things you read are the first time you've ever heard them, then I suggest you throw this book in your travel bag and reread it on long plane rides until it sinks in, as this is the foundation to everything as a polo player.

My dream in polo was "to be able to play with the best polo players in the world, because they asked me to be there." It wasn't about a certain title, or a certain tournament win, or about being a professional player...they were all extremely valuable gifts, necessities and by products along the journey to achieving my original dream and goal. I absolutely conquered my dream and throughout my career I have had the absolute honor to play in 20-26 goal polo as a professional, for some of the greatest players of all time both American and Argentine who hold the longest winning records such as the world's number one player Adolfo Cambiaso, the legendary Carlos Gracida and Memo Gracida, Eduardo Heguy, Pite and Sebastian Merlos, Gonzalito Pieres, Dale Smicklas, Owen Rinehart, Julio Arellano, Adam Snow, Benjamin and Santiago Araya, among others. And I can attest to the fact that there is no other feeling or emotion in the world as an athlete and aspiring professional to get the call from a 10 goal player requesting you to play on their team...and sometimes knowing they dropped a player to bring me on the team. Talk about taking a risk to your sponsor if you were that top professional player. "Hey really...she can play, trust me". To all of them I say a sincere thank you for giving me the chance to do what I came to do, it has been the ride and journey of a lifetime and one I am so appreciative of as it continues to unfold.

I thank God for my unique talent and all of the people involved in helping me achieve my biggest dream on the list so far. Some of the stories of how and when I got the call to play on some of the biggest teams that led to historical wins are absolutely priceless, as I was never the first person listed on the team when the High Goal team rosters were released preseason. I was usually the person who got the call after the season started, which meant no time to practice with the team, just jump in after they were up and rolling...let's do this! What an adrenaline rush and an absolute honor to be able to play with and against some of the greatest players of all time. Each time I walked on the field for one of those games, I knew I had no fear...none. I knew this was the chance I had been waiting for and working so hard towards. I now had the chance to do what I came to do and I was "all in". It was also a complete honor to get to learn from the best players in the world everything I could absorb about the game. Each player I played for and against gave me new insight into different theories and strategies on the same general tasks that are necessary in a polo game. What I can say about this unique opportunity is that each one has a special twist on the best way to go about playing polo, so pay attention to who inspires you and then do some investigating on how they do it.

Thanks for buying the book and hearing what I have to say. I hope you have many things to take away from our conversation that will help elevate your polo and your understanding of what it takes to improve as a player. The bottom line is this…be willing to do the work it takes and get ready for the journey of a lifetime if you do.

I look forward to sharing some more in depth details on some of my absolute favorite topics in polo such as polo horses and strategy, as the Let's Talk Polo book series is released. And for those of you who want to know how I conquered my dream in polo, you will want to look for my other book called "Conquering the Dream". So until then, get to work on what I've lined out here and we'll chat soon!

All the best,

Sunny

www.sunnyhalepolo.com

CHAPTER ELEVEN

Who is Sunny Hale...

ESPNW compares her accomplishments as, "Some say she's pulled off the equivalent of being the first woman to earn a World Series ring."

Sunny is widely recognized as the most accomplished and well-respected female Polo player in the world. What sets her apart from the pack, is her achievements at the top of what has traditionally been a male dominated sport and the fact that she was hired as a professional player to compete on teams alongside some of the greatest male players in the sport for over 20 seasons. Sunny is the first woman in US History to win the prestigious US Open Polo Championships, American Polo's most coveted tournament.

Inducted into the National Cowgirl Hall of Fame
"The women who shape the West change the world."

The NCHF honors and celebrates women, past and present, whose lives exemplify the courage, resilience, and independence that helped shape the American West. Honorees also include: Sandra Day O'Connor, Georgia O'Keeffe, Annie Oakley and Patsy Cline among others.

Wins and special awards in Polo *(partial list)*

7 Time Polo Magazine Woman Player of the Year

US Open 26 goal: Outback Steakhouse Polo Team
Adolfo Cambiaso, Sunny Hale, Lolo Castagnola, Phil Heatly
*Tim Gannon- team patron

CV Whitney Cup 26 goal: Lechuza Caracas Polo Team
Pite Merlos, Sebastian Merlos, Victor Vargas, Sunny Hale

Hall of Fame Cup 22 goal: Outback Steakhouse
Adolfo Cambiaso, Gonzalito Pieres, Sunny Hale, Tim Gannon

Ylvisaker Cup 22 goal & MVP: La Dolfina / Newbridge
Adolfo Cambiaso, Sunny Hale, Matias Magrini, Russ McCall

Sterling Cup 22 goal: Calumet Polo Team
Eduardo Heguy, Nachi Heguy, Henry DK, Sunny Hale

Robert Skene 20 goal: Goshen Polo Team
* voted by players **MVP Robert Skene Award**
Owen Rinehart, Julio Arellano, Sunny Hale, Ervin Abel

Bondell Cup 20 goal: Audi Polo Team
Gonzalito Pieres, Sunny Hale, Melissa Ganzi, Juan Bollini

Texas Open 20 goal & MVP: Bob Moore Cadillac
International Cup 16 goal: Sympatico Polo Team
Palm Beach Polo & Country Club 14 goal League

Wins and special awards in Polo *(partial list)*

Women's Polo:

US Women's Open 1990, 2011, 2013 & MVP

WCT Finals 2006, 2007, 2009, 2010, 2011, 2012

First Royal Malaysian Ladies Polo Championships 2012

USA vs Argentina at Palermo Field #1

ICWI International Ladies Tournament Jamaica

Argentine Women's Open 1999

Thai Polo Queen's Cup 2012

Dubai International Ladies Tournament
 under the patronage of Sheikha Maitha al Maktoum

Win of special note:

Don King Days...the famous buckle!

Organizations Sunny has founded in Polo

WCT (Women's Championship Tournament)

International women's polo league. WCT's mission is new friendships, good polo...shared passion.

www.wctwomenspolo.com

facebook.com/WCTwomenspolo

American Polo Horse Association

Created in 2006 to recognize and document polo ponies.

www.americanpolohorse.com

www.mypolopony.com

facebook.com/AmericanPoloHorse

Made in the USA
Las Vegas, NV
21 February 2021

18291832R00111